Iraq

Iraq

By Liz Sonneborn

Enchantment of the World™
Second Series

Children's Press®

An Imprint of Scholastic Inc.

New York Toronto London Auckland Sydney
Mexico City New Delhi Hong Kong
Danbury, Connecticut

Frontispiece: Kadoumia Mosque, Baghdad

Consultant: Kamran Agahaie, Director of the Center for Middle Eastern Studies, University of Texas–Austin

Please note: All statistics are as up-to-date as possible at the time of publication.

Book production by The Design Lab

Library of Congress Cataloging-in-Publication Data
Sonneborn, Liz.
  Iraq/by Liz Sonneborn.
     p. cm.—(Enchantment of the world. Second series)
  Includes bibliographical references and index.
  ISBN-13: 978-0-531-25312-0 (lib. bdg.)
  ISBN-10: 0-531-25312-0 (lib. bdg.)
  1. Iraq—Juvenile literature. I. Title. II. Series.
  DS70.62.S63 2012
  956.7—dc23   2011032218

SCHOLASTIC, CHILDREN'S PRESS, and associated logos are trademarks and/or registered trademarks of Scholastic Inc.
1 2 3 4 5 6 7 8 9 10 R 21 20 19 18 17 16 15 14 13 12

Iraq

Contents

Cover photo:
A mosque in
Baghdad

Qandil Mountains

Apollo butterfly

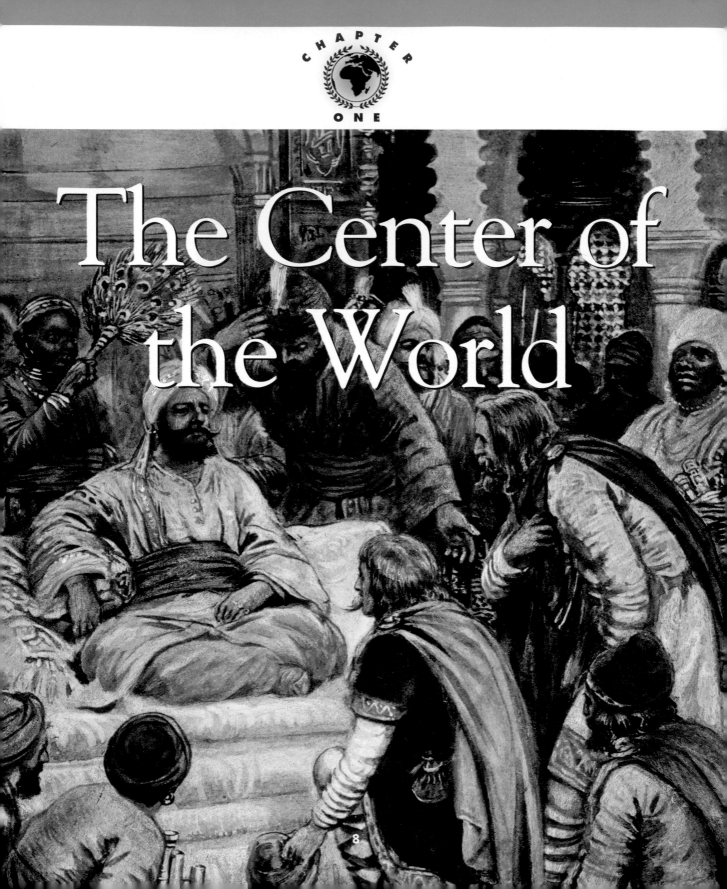

The Center of the World

8.

IN 762, ABU JAFAR AL-MANSUR SENT A TEAM OF SCOUTS on a mission. They were told to find the ideal place for the new capital of the vast Abbasid Empire. At the time, the Abbasids controlled lands throughout southwestern Asia and northern Africa. As the new Abbasid caliph, or ruler, al-Mansur wanted a capital that would glorify his family by showing all the world the extent of the Abbasids' wealth and power.

Opposite: **Baghdad was the center of a great empire. Here, the caliph, or leader of the empire, receives a representative from Charlemagne, the Holy Roman emperor in Europe.**

The City of Peace

After a thorough investigation, al-Mansur found just the right spot for his glorious city. It was on the west bank of the Tigris River, which flows through what is now the country of Iraq. The location had a lot of benefits. It was in the center of the Abbasid Empire and close to established trade routes. For the region, the climate was comfortable. The Tigris could provide a reliable source of water as well as a means of shipping goods in and out. The area also featured some of the most fertile land in the empire, ensuring that nearby farms could feed a large population.

Al-Mansur spared no expense on his project. He hired architects, engineers, and artisans from all over the world to design his city. The caliph also enlisted the services of Naubakht, an Iranian astrologer. He consulted his astrological charts to determine the best month to begin construction. To ensure the city's good fortune, Naubakht announced that work should begin in July, under the astrological sign of Leo, represented by the strong and noble lion.

Some one hundred thousand laborers descended on the Tigris. For four years, they worked to create al-Mansur's vision. They built three great circular walls around the city center to keep it safe from invaders. The walls gave the city its nickname, Round City. But al-Mansur had another name for it:

A bronze head of Abu Jafar al-Mansur sits in west Baghdad, honoring the founder of the city. It is 16 feet (5 m) high.

Baghdad was the center of the world during the time of the Abbasids.

Dar al-Salam, meaning "city of peace." He was thrilled by his majestic capital. On seeing Dar al-Salam, he declared, "This is indeed the city that I am to found, where I am to live, and where my descendants will reign afterward."

The Royal Palace

The residents of Dar al-Salam called it by a different name. The site where it was built had housed the small village of Baghdad. Baghdad quickly became the unofficial name of the Abbasids' beautiful capital city.

Within the city walls, the most spectacular building was the palace of the caliph. Called Bab al-Dhahab (golden gate), it was made of marble and topped by an enormous green dome. The interior was decorated with gold paint, colorful tapestries, and silk wall hangings. The furniture was the finest

Fine pottery was made during the Abbasid Empire. This bowl dates to the ninth century.

made. Everywhere, there were decorative objects crafted from gold and silver and vases imported from China.

The palace grounds were surrounded by gardens, adorned with fountains and sculptures. The caliph even had a private zoo full of exotic wild animals. In front of the palace was a large open square. Tournaments, races, and other amusements were staged there. Daily, it was the site of a parade held by members of the Abbasids' army. Teams of workers kept the four wide roads that led out of the city clean and free of litter. At night, lamps brightly lit the square and the roads.

A Growing Capital

The capital soon outgrew the city walls. The caliph gave grants of land nearby to government workers, soldiers, family, and

The Tigris River flows through Baghdad, connecting it to distant parts of the world.

friends. As Baghdad prospered, more and more people came to live there. Within a generation, the city had expanded to both sides of the Tigris.

Baghdad attracted people from all walks of life. Its residents were merchants, artists, goldsmiths, reed weavers, booksellers, and soap makers. Its giant open-air markets offered all types of goods—from food to flowers to textiles. Baghdad soon became one of the most important centers for trade and commerce in the world. Every day, the Tigris was full of ships ready to transport goods made in Baghdad to ports far away.

At its height in the ninth century, Baghdad was home to as many as half a million people. It was one of the largest and most sophisticated cities in the region. It had a diverse population, with residents from a wide array of geographic, ethnic, and religious backgrounds. The Abbasids were descended from Muhammad, the Prophet of Islam. Although they were Muslim leaders, they allowed non-Muslims to worship however they chose, provided they accepted the political authority of the Muslim rulers.

The House of Wisdom

The caliphs who succeeded al-Mansur wanted Baghdad to be more than a hub for international trade. Al-Ma'mun, who reigned from 813 to 833, was particularly determined to turn the capital into a center for culture and learning. In 830, he estab-

The House of Wisdom helped to translate many important documents, such as this description of the anatomy of the eye.

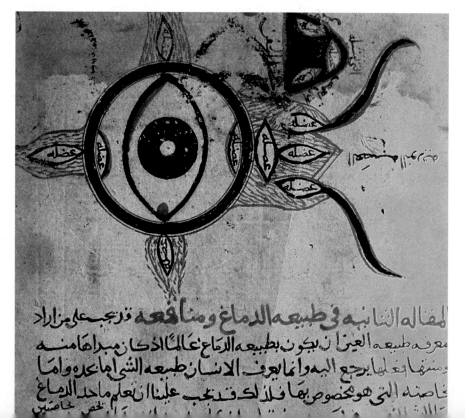

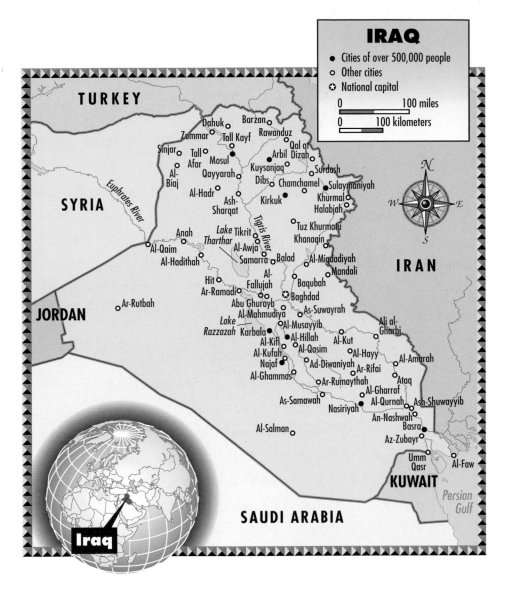

lished the Bayt al-Hikma, or House of Wisdom. He brought scholars from around the world to this institution. They were charged with translating religious and philosophical texts from other places and civilizations into Arabic, the most important language of scholarship and education in the Abbasid Empire. The translations were then cataloged and stored in the caliph's library. Because of the Bayt al-Hikma, many ancient books that otherwise might have been lost forever were preserved for future generations. For example, were it not for the House of Wisdom, the works of the Greek philosophers Plato and Aristotle would be largely unknown today.

Al-Ma'mun soon expanded the Bayt al-Hikma's mission. He invited scholars of science and mathematics to come to Baghdad. There, they shared their knowledge and research with one another. In this way, the Bayt al-Hikma helped advance many different fields of study, including medicine, engineering, philosophy, mathematics, and astronomy.

The Sacking of Baghdad

As centuries passed, the Abbasids suffered from political power struggles and religious and ethnic strife. Although the empire became increasingly decentralized, Baghdad kept its reputation as a capital of world culture. Its glory days, however, came to a horrific end in 1258, when a Mongol army from central Asia invaded the city. The Mongols destroyed Baghdad's magnificent buildings, burned its libraries, and tossed into the Tigris the books that stored so much of the world's knowledge. Worse still, the Mongols slaughtered hundreds of thousands of residents. Many leading scholars and even the caliph were put to death during the sacking of Baghdad.

But the story of Baghdad did not end there. Although it was no longer a sparkling metropolis, the city survived. As the centuries passed, the people of Baghdad were forced to weather many more disasters, from droughts to political unrest and foreign invasions. But when the modern country of Iraq was founded in 1932, Baghdad, the largest city in the new nation, became its capital.

Since that time, both Baghdad and Iraq have faced enormous challenges and suffered extraordinary difficulties. But the Iraqi people have remained as strong as they are proud. Memories of Baghdad's illustrious past as the greatest city in the world only help to fuel their hopes for a brilliant future for their beloved, but troubled country.

Despite the recent violence, some of Baghdad's beautiful mosques and monuments have survived.

Land Between the Rivers

IRAQ IS LOCATED IN SOUTHWESTERN ASIA IN A REGION
known as the Middle East. It shares borders with six other
countries. Turkey lies to the north; Syria, Jordan, and Saudi
Arabia to the west; Kuwait to the south; and Iran to the east.
Iraq covers an area of 169,235 square miles (438,317 square
kilometers), making it about the same size as the state of
California.

Iraq is almost entirely landlocked. Its only bit of coastline
is found in the extreme southeastern portion of the country,
sandwiched between Kuwait and Iran. Measuring just 22 miles
(35 km) long, this coastline gives Iraq access to the large
body of water known as the Persian Gulf, which is sometimes
referred to as the Arabian Gulf.

Opposite: **The Euphrates River begins in Turkey, crosses Syria, and runs through central Iraq. The Tigris and Euphrates Rivers have long helped Iraq flourish.**

The Tigris and Euphrates

Running nearly the length of Iraq are two great rivers: the
Tigris and the Euphrates. These rivers have been enormously
important throughout the history of Iraq. In ancient times,

Iraq's Geographic Features

Highest Elevation: Cheekha Dar, 11,847 feet (3,611 m) above sea level

Lowest Elevation: Persian Gulf, sea level

Longest River: Euphrates River, about 660 miles (1,060 km) in Iraq

Largest Lake: Lake Tharthar, 1,050 square miles (2,720 sq km)

Largest City: Baghdad, 5,402,486 people (2010 est.)

Longest Border: With Iran, 906 miles (1,458 km)

Shortest Border: With Jordan, 112 miles (180 km)

Hottest Month: August, average high temperature of 111°F (44°C)

Coldest Month: January, average low temperature of 39°F (4°C)

Hottest Recorded Temperature: 125°F (52°C), on June 14, 2010, in Basra

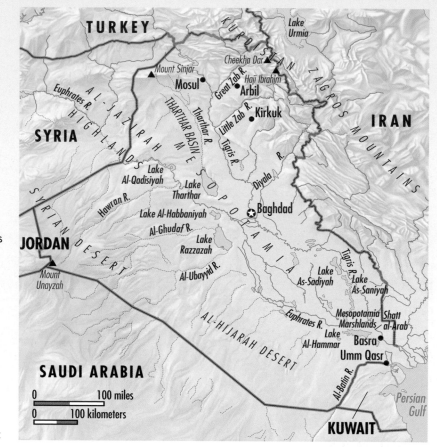

they gave the region its name, Mesopotomia, which meant "land between the rivers" in the ancient Greek language.

The Euphrates is the longest river in Iraq. Measuring 1,740 miles (2,800 km) long, it originates in Turkey and flows through Syria before reaching Iraq. The Euphrates, however, is fairly shallow. The Tigris is much deeper and therefore easier for ships and boats to navigate. On the Tigris, ships from the Persian Gulf can travel all the way to the capital city of Baghdad in central Iraq.

Every spring, during Iraq's rainy season, the waters of the Tigris and Euphrates rise. Traditionally, they overflowed their banks, flooding the surrounding soil. The yearly floods made the river valleys into fertile farmlands. These areas are still heavily farmed, but the waters are now controlled by a system of modern dams and reservoirs.

Haditha Dam limits the flow of the Euphrates. The dam produces electricity and provides water for irrigation.

In southeastern Iraq, the Tigris and Euphrates merge about 68 miles (109 km) north of the Persian Gulf. The wide waterway these rivers form there is called the Shatt al-Arab (meaning "coast of the Arabs"). The area along the Shatt al-Arab is full of lakes and marshes—lowlands that are usually waterlogged.

Deserts and Mountains

Most of Iraq is far drier than the Shatt al-Arab region. In fact, much of the country's territory to the south and west are desert lands. It is so hot and dry in the Iraqi deserts that very few people live there.

The Marsh Arabs

For thousands of years, the marsh dwellers, who are now referred to as Marsh Arabs, have inhabited the wetlands of southern Iraq near the Iranian border. By carefully bundling the reeds that grew wild in the area's marshes, they built sturdy homes that are called *mudhifs* in Arabic. The wildlife in the marshes provided them with their food and livelihood. The Marsh Arabs made their living by fishing, hunting, and herding the water buffalo native to the region.

In the 1990s, however, the Marsh Arabs' traditional way of life was threatened. They had participated in an attempt to overthrow the government of Iraqi dictator Saddam Hussein. To get revenge, Hussein had the marshes drained, forcing the Marsh Arabs to abandon their homes. By draining the marshes, Hussein also destroyed the natural habitat of many species of birds and other wildlife.

Since 2003, when Saddam Hussein was removed from power, groups such as Nature Iraq have been working to bring back the marshes. About 30 percent of the marshes have been restored. Slowly, both people and wildlife native to the marshes are returning home.

Most desert residents are Bedouins, who make up about 2 percent of Iraq's population. They generally live in portable tents and make their living by raising livestock, especially sheep and goats. The Bedouins are nomadic. To provide water for their animals, they travel along well-established routes in the desert from one pasture or watering hole to another. These watering holes are wells or riverbeds, called wadis, that collect the little rain that falls in the Iraqi desert.

The terrain of northeastern Iraq, along its borders with Turkey and Iran, provides a stark contrast to the country's forbidding desert lands. This area features some of the most beautiful and dramatic landscapes found in Iraq, including deep canyons, stirring waterfalls, and majestic mountains. The

The rugged Qandil Mountains lie in Kurdistan, along the border between Iraq and Iran.

Urban Iraq

The biggest city in Iraq is its capital, Baghdad. But much of the country's largely urban population lives in the many other cities located throughout Iraq.

Far to the north is Mosul (below). Located near the upper reaches of the Tigris River, it is the second-largest city in Iraq, with an estimated population of 2,882,442. It is also Iraq's most ethnically diverse urban area. Its population includes Kurds, Assyrians, Turkmens, Yazidis, and other ethnic minorities. Mosul has the largest number of Christians of any Iraqi city. It also has a strong mix of Sunnis and Shi'is, the two main sects, or groups, in Islam. Across the Tigris from Mosul are the ruins of Nineveh. This ancient city was the capital of the Assyrian Empire.

Basra, Iraq's chief port and third-largest city, has an estimated population of 1,914,205. It is located in southern Iraq on the Shatt al-Arab. Because of its access to the Persian Gulf, Basra historically has been an

important center for trade. It is also central to Iraq's oil industry. About one thousand oil wells surround the city.

The city of Arbil, Iraq's fourth-largest city, lies about 50 miles (80 km) east of Mosul. At the center of the city is an ancient elevated mound called Arbil Citadel (above). People have been living on this site for five thousand years. Traditionally, Arbil was an important center for trade along the route linking Mosul and Baghdad. It is today the chief city in Iraqi Kurdistan, the area in Iraq ruled largely by Kurds, who make up the largest ethnic group in the region. Arbil is Iraq's fastest-growing city. Its skyline features the Korek Tower, the tallest building in Iraq.

Kirkuk, Iraq's fifth-largest city, is located near Iraq's border with Iran in the foothills of the Zagros Mountains. Kirkuk is Iraq's most oil-rich city.

region's highest peaks are part of the Zagros Mountains. Some rise nearly 12,000 feet (3,600 meters) high. In mountainous areas in northern and eastern Iraq, nomads travel to high altitudes in the hot summers and back down to lower altitudes during the colder winter months.

Iraq's Climate

The temperature and weather in Iraq are just as varied as its landscapes. Not surprisingly, the hottest areas in Iraq are its desert lands. There, temperatures often rise to 120 degrees Fahrenheit (49 degrees Celsius) in the summer. The desert is also very dry. It receives only a few inches of rainfall a year. As a result, sandstorms are common in the Iraqi desert. During a sandstorm, heavy winds fill the air with clouds of sand.

Weather in the Tigris and Euphrates River valleys can also be harsh. In Baghdad, summer temperatures can rise as high as 122°F (50°C). Winters, however, are fairly mild. In the cooler months, the capital enjoys an average daily temperature of about 52°F (11°C).

In the mountainous northeast, winters are frigid. The temperature is often below freezing, and heavy snows are common in higher elevations. As the weather warms, melting mountain snow flows south, often causing extensive flooding in central Iraq. Summers in the northwest, however, are very comfortable, especially in contrast to the stifling heat in much of Iraq. In part because of its pleasant summer weather, northeastern Iraq is becoming a favorite vacation spot for tourists across the Middle East.

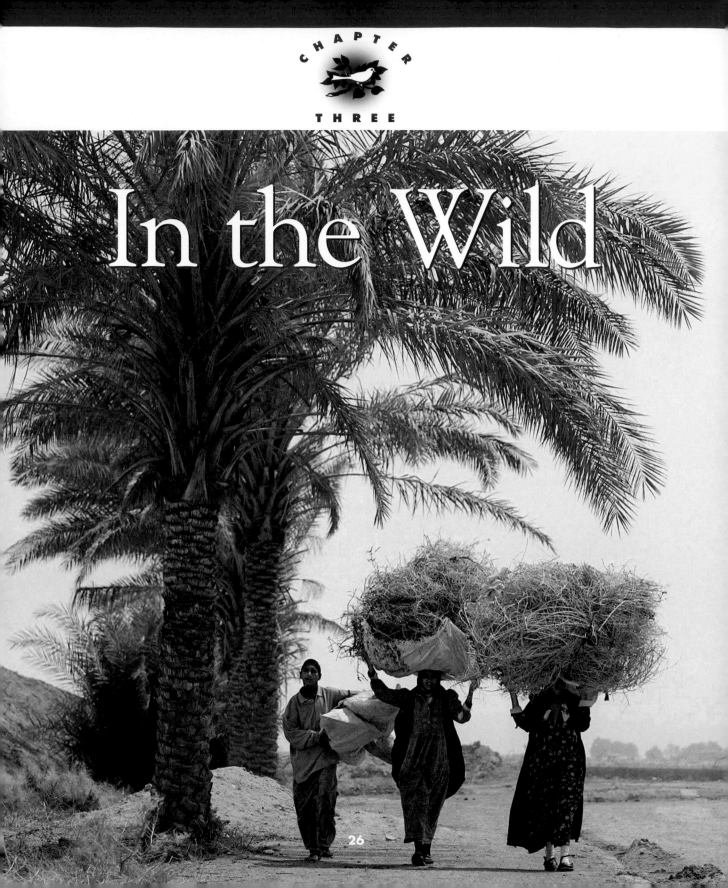

In the Wild

W ITH ITS VARIED LANDSCAPE, IT IS NO SURPRISE THAT
the plants and animals that live in Iraq differ greatly from place
to place. The moist and often temperate mountain region is a
hospitable habitat for many species. But the vast deserts that
cover much of Iraq are home to only the hardiest of creatures.

Opposite: **Palm trees thrive in many parts of Iraq.**

Plant Life

With little water and extreme heat, few plants survive in the
desert lands. But a handful of species are well adapted to the
grueling conditions. Tall orchard grass, for instance, grows
well under drought conditions, although it fares best in the
cooler months. The rose of Jericho is also common in the
desert. From December to April, when modest rains fall, this
shrub decorates the desert with its small white blooms.

The banks of the Tigris and Euphrates Rivers provide a
much friendlier environment for plant life. Many wild grasses
and plants thrive there. They include willows, tamarisks,
poplars, and bullrushes. Licorice plants also flourish near the

The Rose of Jericho

The deserts of Iraq are home to a variety of flowering plants, including the rose of Jericho. This plant is well adapted to an extremely hot and dry environment. During times of little rain, its leaves droop and die, forming a protective ball around the plant's fruits, which hold its seeds. When rains return, the leaves unfurl so the seeds can be scattered, producing new plants.

rivers. Their thick roots are used to make a juice that flavors licorice candies.

The fertile soil of the river valleys makes the region the center of Iraqi agriculture. Farmers there plant many different crops. Grains such as wheat, barley, and flax grow especially well in the area. The access to water also makes the Tigris-Euphrates valleys excellent places to raise livestock. Cattle, sheep, goats, and pigs all thrive in this region.

Southern Iraq, where the Tigris and Euphrates meet, is dotted with lakes and marshes. These areas support grasses, rushes, and reeds. Among the flowering plants native to this region are sedges, pimpernels, and geraniums.

With its fertile soil and plentiful supply of water, Iraq's mountainous region to the northeast is particularly hospitable to plants. The country's only forests are found there. On the lower slopes grow hawthorns, willows, pines, and other varieties of trees. Large forests of oak trees were once a feature of the area, but so many oaks were cut down for lumber that the forests are now much smaller.

The Birds of Iraq

The most frequently sighted animals in Iraq are birds. About four hundred species of birds make their home there. Some live in Iraq year-round, while others make yearly migrations into the country to breed.

One common bird of Iraq is the marbled duck, known by its blotchy white-and-brown feathers. About forty thousand of these ducks are found in the southern marshes. The white-eared bulbul also lives in the south. These small birds get their name from the large white spot on the sides of their black heads.

Once feared extinct, the sacred ibis has recently been seen in southern Iraq. These beautiful birds with white wings and black heads were revered in ancient Egypt. The Egyptian god Thoth had the head of an ibis.

Growing Dates

Several decades ago, southern Iraq had more than thirty million date palms. Each year, these trees produced about 1 million metric tons of dates. The sweet, sticky fruits are a favorite treat throughout the Middle East. Iraq once exported more dates than any other country in the world, but after years of war, as many as half of Iraq's date palms have died. The date industry has also dwindled. Many people who used to work in the orchards left to take government jobs that paid better.

Recently, the Iraqi government has begun working to revive the country's date industry. It has an ambitious plan to increase the number of date palms in the country to forty million by about 2020.

Birds found in northern Iraq include the cinereous bunting, the lesser white-fronted goose, and the Egyptian vulture. Even Iraq's desert lands support a few bird species. For instance, the slight cream-colored courser survives there on a diet of insects.

Mammals Large and Small

Iraq is home to about 75 species of wild mammals. Most are small animals, such as badgers, muskrats, porcupines, and otters. The country also has about fifteen different species of bats.

Some of Iraq's larger mammals include wolves, foxes, hyenas, and boars. In the mountains, brown bears and sometimes even leopards can be seen. Iraqis living in the marshes often maintain herds of water buffalo, while hunters there stalk wild jackals and gazelles.

Badgers spend much of their time in underground homes called setts. Setts sometimes have 300 feet (90 m) of tunnels with forty entrances.

The Basra Reed Warbler

Among the rare birds found in Iraq is the Basra reed warbler. Identifiable by its distinctive yellow belly and dark eye stripe, the brown-feathered warbler traditionally spent the winter in East Africa, but returned each year to Iraq to breed. Its accustomed breeding ground was located in the marshes along the Iran-Iraq border. There, the warbler built deep nests from local grass among the reeds that flourished in these wetlands.

During the 1990s, the marshes were drained, nearly destroying the warbler's natural habitat. Still, the Basra reed warbler survived. Some of the birds successfully sought new breeding grounds as far away as Israel. Recently, however, they have begun returning to Iraq. Conservation groups and the new Iraqi government have been working to save and restore the marshes and to protect the wildlife that makes the wetlands its home.

Fish, Reptiles, and Insects

Dozens of types of freshwater fish swim in Iraq's rivers and lakes. Carp and catfish are often caught. Carp from the Tigris is a favorite with Iraqi diners. It is the main ingredient in *masgouf*, the national dish of Iraq.

Reptiles and insects are found throughout Iraq, even in the most punishing desert habitats. The spiny-tailed lizard, for example, is common in hot, dry areas. One of the most feared animals in Iraq is the Levantine viper, whose bite can kill humans, horses, and even camels. Iraqi insects include locusts, dragonflies, and butterflies. There are perhaps as many as three hundred varieties of butterflies in Iraq, including the rare Apollo butterfly, which is sometimes seen in the mountains of Kurdistan.

Egyptian spiny-tailed lizards, which live throughout much of the Middle East, can be found in dry, rocky areas. Bedouins sometimes used their skin to make leather.

The Apollo butterfly has bright red spots, which fade as the creature ages, so they eventually look orange.

Protecting Natural Iraq

During the reign of Iraqi dictator Saddam Hussein (1979–2003), the government did little to protect the country's natural habitats. In fact, its decision to drain the southern marshlands almost destroyed this ecosystem and drove away much of its native wildlife. According to the United Nations, an international peacekeeping organization, the destruction of Iraq's marshes was one of the greatest environmental disasters of the twentieth century.

Since the fall of Hussein, several people and groups have begun working to restore and preserve Iraq's natural spaces. Among them is Ihsan Al-Shehbaz. He is a botanist, a scientist who studies plants. He is compiling a catalog that records all the vegetation native to Iraq. Al-Shehbaz also hopes to establish a botanical garden that showcases the plant life of his country.

Another person concerned with preserving Iraq's natural world is engineer and environmentalist Azzam Alwash. During Saddam Hussein's rule, Alwash lived in the United States. But after the dictator was removed from power, Alwash returned to Iraq to see how he could help his ailing country.

The Baghdad Zoo

When a U.S.-led coalition of troops invaded Baghdad in 2003, among the earliest casualties were hundreds of animals housed in a zoo there. During the military takeover of Baghdad, some animals escaped. Others died of hunger and thirst after being left unattended. Still others were stolen by looters, who slaughtered many of the animals for food. Only a few dozen of the zoo animals survived the ordeal.

Since that time, the Baghdad Zoo has been rebuilt and opened to the public. Now it provides a home for more than one thousand animals, including tigers, bears, gazelles, and jaguars. One of the most popular attractions in Iraq, the zoo welcomes millions of visitors each year.

Azzam Alwash is working to restore Iraq's marshlands and hopes to establish protected areas throughout the country.

He has since founded Nature Iraq. The organization first concerned itself with working to restore the marshlands. It has since broadened its mission to protecting other areas in Iraq where development or neglect might threaten the native habitat. Alwash is seeking government help in creating a national park in the marshlands and establishing formal protection for Mount Permagrone in Kurdistan, which is home to one-sixth of all species of plant life in Iraq. In 2010, Alwash explained to the *Christian Science Monitor*, "If I want the marshes restored and managed properly, I have to not only protect the marshes but protect the integrity of the environment in Kurdistan because it's all one habitat."

Boys fish in a marsh near Karbala, 50 miles (80 km) south of Baghdad.

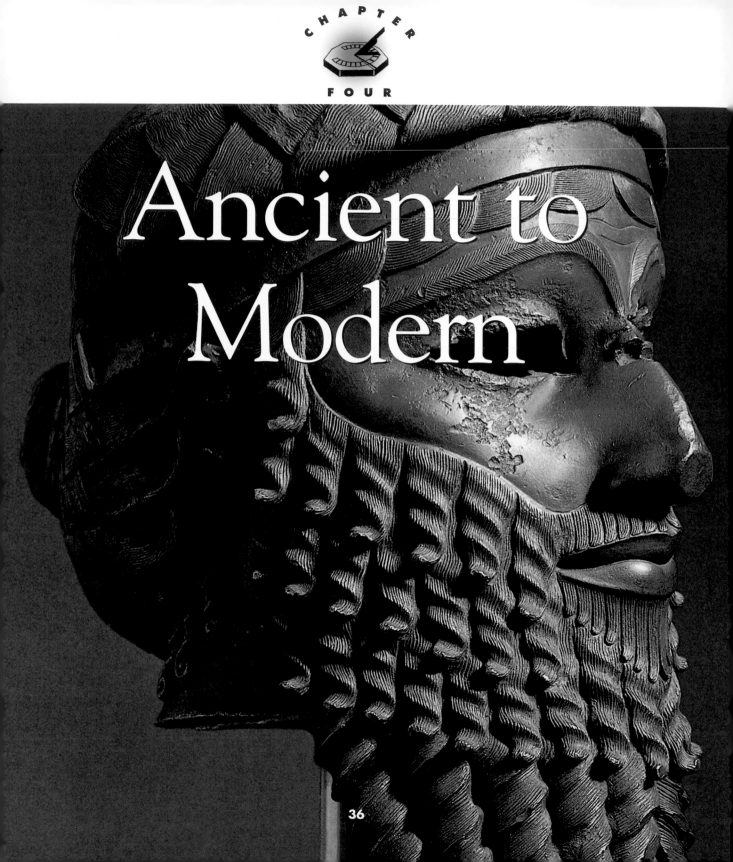

Ancient to Modern

THE TIGRIS AND EUPHRATES RIVER VALLEYS OF present-day Iraq have often been called the Cradle of Civilization. It was there that many of the greatest civilizations of the ancient world were born. At different times in history, Iraq was at the center of mighty empires that controlled vast lands and enormous populations.

Under Many Empires

Six thousand years ago, the Sumerian civilization grew up in central Iraq. The Sumerians learned to cultivate crops on the land watered by Iraq's two great rivers. But that was far from the Sumerians' only achievement. They were also the first people to discover how to use the wheel and to develop metalworking. They also created the first accurate calendars and invented the concept of an hour. And, most importantly, they developed the first known form of writing. By writing on clay tablets in a script now called cuneiform, the Sumerians became the earliest people to keep a written record of their own history.

Iraq and the Bible

Legend places many important sites in the Bible in what is now Iraq. The Garden of Eden, where Adam and Eve are said to have lived, was supposedly located between the Tigris and Euphrates Rivers. The Tower of Babel (right), which figures in the story of how humankind acquired different languages, was also said to be in the country. The ancient city of Ur, located near the contemporary Iraqi city of Nasiriyah, was identified as the hometown of Abraham, a prominent religious figure for Muslims, Christians, and Jews.

The Sumerian Empire eventually gave way to Babylonia, the next great civilization in Iraq. In about 1792 BCE, Hammurabi became the Babylonian ruler. He developed the Code of Hammurabi, the first written collection of laws ever produced.

The Code of Hammurabi was carved into a large stone monument.

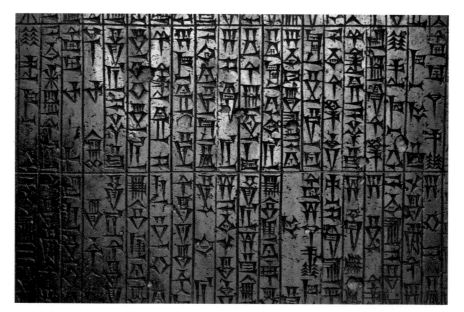

The Great Ziggurat of Ur

Visitors to the Dhi Qar Province in Iraq can see a monument to the region's glorious past—the Great Ziggurat of Ur. Sumerian people built this structure about four thousand years ago during the reign of Ur-Nammu.

Constructed throughout ancient Mesopotamia, ziggurats were towers built in steps. A temple was often placed on the top. Made out of mud bricks, the Great Ziggurat of Ur honored the Sumerian moon god Nanna. Originally, it was more than 100 feet (30 m) tall, and its base measured about 30,000 square feet (2,800 sq m).

Over many centuries, the ziggurat began to crumble. When it was almost in ruins, Nabonidus, the last king of the Babylonian Empire, had it rebuilt in the sixth century BCE. Today, it is one of the best-preserved ziggurats in the world.

As Babylonian power declined, the Assyrian Empire rose to take its place. Its capital, Nineveh, was home to a great library of cuneiform writing and an enclosed garden watered through irrigation. The Babylonian king Nabopolassar recaptured Iraq in 612 BCE. His son, Nebuchadnezzar II, is responsible for creating the fabulous Hanging Gardens of Babylon. Called one of the Seven Wonders of the World, the gardens were planted on a series of tiered terraces within the walls surrounding the royal palace.

In the sixth century BCE, Cyrus the Great of the Persian Achaemenian Empire—based in what is now Iran—invaded and conquered Iraq. Over the next thousand years, the region

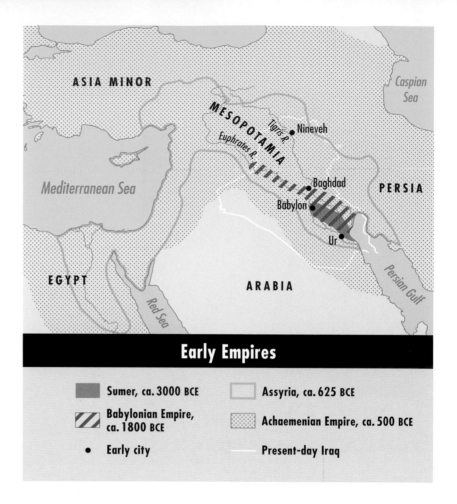

Early Empires

- **Sumer, ca. 3000 BCE**
- **Babylonian Empire, ca. 1800 BCE**
- **Early city**
- **Assyria, ca. 625 BCE**
- **Achaemenian Empire, ca. 500 BCE**
- **Present-day Iraq**

frequently changed hands, as other conquerors were attracted by the fertile lands along the Tigris and Euphrates. At different times, the area came under the control of various empires, including those of the Seleucids, the Parthians, and the Sassanid Persians.

The Muslim Empire

In the seventh century CE, the followers of a prophet named Muhammad, called Muslims, began gaining authority in the region. Their religion of Islam slowly spread, and within a few centuries, Muslims became the majority in the region. This slow conversion to Islam had an important long-term impact on the Middle East, where caliphs (Muslim leaders) began to rule a vast empire. The Muslim Empire eventually stretched from central Asia to what is now Spain.

By 638, nearly all of Iraq had been conquered by the Arab Muslims. They established several cities—including Basra and Mosul—that still exist today. Although its fertile lands made the area the most prosperous in the empire, most of the early caliphs of the Muslim Umayyad dynasty neglected Iraq. The people in the region were unhappy under the rule of the Umayyads and rose up against them several times, including in 701, but the rebellions were unsuccessful.

Basra became a center of learning and a large library was built there.

About fifty years later, the Abbasids, a family that claimed to be directly descended from the Prophet Muhammad, challenged the Umayyads. When the Abbasids' armies reached Iraq, the population threw their support to these new leaders.

In 749, Abu al-Abbas was named the first caliph of the Abbasids in the city of Kufah in south-central Iraq. The Abbasids ruled from Kufah until 762, when a new caliph, al-Mansur, moved the capital of the empire to Baghdad. Under his rule, the old village there was transformed into one of the largest and most impressive cities in the world. During its height in the eighth and ninth centuries, it was a leading center of commerce, culture, and scholarship.

After that time, Baghdad gradually began to decline politically. Tensions between various peoples in the region led to political instability, but the Abbasids managed to maintain control. The worst blow came in 1258, when a Mongol army led by Hulagu Khan invaded Baghdad. The Mongols destroyed much of the city and killed many of its residents.

In 1533, Iraq was taken over by the Ottomans, who

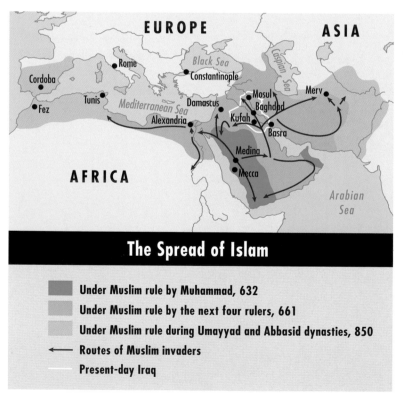

The Spread of Islam

- Under Muslim rule by Muhammad, 632
- Under Muslim rule by the next four rulers, 661
- Under Muslim rule during Umayyad and Abbasid dynasties, 850
- ← Routes of Muslim invaders
- — Present-day Iraq

Looking at Light

Alhazen, who lived from about 965 to 1040, was one of the most inventive scientists of his day. Born in the Iraqi city of Basra, Alhazen spent most of his life in Cairo, Egypt. He wrote many books, including seven on optics, the study of light and human sight. Alhazen's works on optics were later translated into Latin and Italian. His ideas had an enormous influence on scientists around the world for hundreds of years. Today, Alhazen's picture appears on Iraq's 10,000-dinar bill.

ruled an empire that was centered in what is now Turkey. Iraq remained part of the Ottoman Empire for hundreds of years. By the nineteenth century, Iraqi Muslims of the Sunni sect joined the Ottoman army in large numbers, and in the process began to gain political influence.

Under British Rule

World War I began in 1914. Many countries took part in this war. The Ottoman Empire was on one side of this conflict, and Great Britain was on the other. During the war, Britain sent a military force to occupy Iraq. The war ended in 1918, and the Ottoman Empire was on the losing side. The empire was broken up, and most of its territories were taken over by European nations.

The League of Nations, an organization set up after the war to secure international peace, drew up Iraq's borders and gave the British control over the new country in 1920. The

Oil gushes out of a well near Kirkuk in 1932. Today, the Kirkuk region still produces about one million barrels of oil a day.

British installed Faisal I as Iraq's king, but the British continued to have influence over Iraq's politics and economy. Many Iraqis, however, strongly opposed British rule over Iraq and demanded more control over their own affairs. The modern state of Iraq came into being in 1932, when it was finally granted independence.

The Rise of Saddam Hussein

Governing modern Iraq proved an enormous challenge. People from many different ethnic and religious groups lived within its borders, and they were unhappy sharing power with one another. For decades, Iraq's government was overseen by Nuri al-Said, who served as prime minister. Said wanted to modernize Iraq and was generally supportive of the influence of Western nations, such as Great Britain. For its part, Great Britain tried to maintain influence over the Iraqi government because, in 1927, oil had been discovered near the northern city of Kirkuk. The British wanted control of this valuable resource.

In 1958, military leaders staged a coup, or overthrow, of the Iraqi government. Both King Faisal II and prime minister Said were murdered. In the coup's aftermath, General Abd al-Karim Qasim was named president, and the country was renamed the Republic of Iraq. Just five years later, another coup brought to power Abdul Salam Arif and later his brother Abdul Rahman Arif—who was, in turn, overthrown by the Arab Socialist Ba'ath Party in 1968.

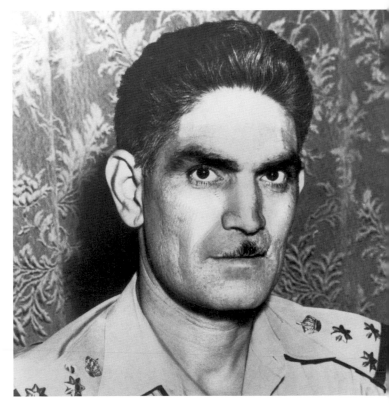

Abd al-Karim Qasim took power following the 1958 coup.

In the 1970s, Ba'ath-dominated government took over the oil industry and used oil profits to fund education, health care, and the building of roads and bridges. As the country thrived, Baghdad grew into a modern city.

This prosperity came to an end when, in 1979, Saddam Hussein became the president of Iraq. He executed many of his political enemies and repressed any group that opposed his rule. Under his regime, Arab Sunni Muslims were given the most important positions in government, and Kurds and Arab Shi'is were given few positions of power. This angered the Kurds, an ethnic group concentrated in northern Iraq, and the Shi'i Arabs, who made up the majority of the Iraqi population.

A year after Hussein took power, the Iraqi army invaded Iran. Iran was in a state of confusion because its government had just been overthrown in a revolution. Because Iran was dominated by Shi'i Muslims, Hussein feared that the Shi'i majority in Iraq might be inspired to rise up against him unless he took action.

The war was a disaster for Iraq. It stretched on for eight long years. The conflict was an enormous drain both in financial and human terms. The war cost many billions of dollars, and hundreds of thousands of Iraqi soldiers and civilians died. In the end, the war achieved little, and the border between Iraq and Iran remained mostly unchanged.

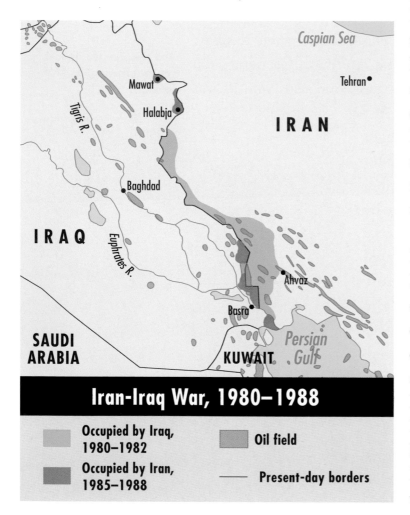

Iran-Iraq War, 1980–1988

Occupied by Iraq, 1980–1982

Occupied by Iran, 1985–1988

Oil field

—— Present-day borders

Terror in Halabja

During the Iran-Iraq War, many Kurds sided with Iran because of their opposition to Saddam Hussein's rule. In the war's closing months, Hussein decided to punish the Kurds in the rural village of Halabja, which was located near the Iran-Iraq border. On the evening of March 16, 1988, military planes began dropping canisters filled with chemical explosives on Halabja. The poisonous gases that were unleashed killed as many as five thousand villagers that day, and thousands more died later. The horrific images of the dead at Halabja have become a symbol of the brutality under Saddam Hussein. In 2003, the Monument of Halabja Martyrs (left) was built where the attack occurred.

The Persian Gulf War

Two years after the end of the Iran-Iraq War, Saddam Hussein sent troops into another neighboring country. This time, his army invaded Kuwait, a small, oil-rich country to the south of Iraq. Kuwait's forces were quickly overwhelmed, and Hussein declared that Kuwait was now part of Iraq.

This action was condemned around the world. With backing from the United Nations (UN), thirty-four countries formed a coalition, or alliance, to force the Iraqis out of Kuwait. After weeks of bombings and ground operations, Iraq's army retreated in February 1991.

Following the conflict, known as the Persian Gulf War, the UN demanded that Iraq stop developing chemical and nuclear weapons, called weapons of mass destruction. It also

Kurdish rebels fire rocket launchers during the 1991 uprising. The rebels gained control of most of northern Iraq before the uprising was brutally crushed.

imposed sanctions on Iraq. The sanctions prohibited nations represented in the UN from trading goods for Iraqi oil. The sanctions were meant to punish and control Saddam Hussein, but they ended up hurting the Iraqi people. Unable to import such necessities as food and medical supplies, many Iraqis suffered and even died.

The coalition forces also implied that they would help the Iraqi people if they staged a popular uprising against Saddam Hussein. Heartened by the promise, many Shi'is and Kurds took up arms against their ruler, but the coalition withdrew instead of coming to their aid. Hussein was ruthless in dealing with the rebels. Many thousands were rounded up, imprisoned, tortured, and killed.

Invading Iraq

On September 11, 2001, two planes flew into the World Trade Center buildings in New York City. Another plane crashed into the Pentagon near Washington, D.C., and still another crashed in a Pennsylvania field before reaching its target. Nearly three thousand people were murdered in these terrorist attacks. Within hours, news reports identified the Middle Eastern terrorist organization al-Qaeda as responsible. The administration of U.S. president George W. Bush immediately began making plans on how to respond. One idea was to attack Iraq.

In the months to come, the Bush administration tried to draw links between al-Qaeda and Saddam Hussein's regime. Most experts, however, believed that there were none. The administration floated other reasons to invade Iraq. It rightly claimed that Hussein was a brutal dictator who oppressed his people. The administration said that for the good of the Iraqi people,

In the 1990s, United Nations inspectors found equipment for making biological weapons in Iraq.

the international community needed to remove him from power. It also maintained that Iraq was producing weapons of mass destruction, violating the Persian Gulf War treaty. Most experts, including UN weapons inspectors, dispute this.

The United States and Great Britain pulled together a force to invade Iraq and remove Hussein from power. The war began in March 2003, and in less than two months U.S. troops entered Baghdad. Saddam Hussein had already fled to avoid capture. He was later caught, tried, and executed.

Saddam Hussein was tried for war crimes and crimes against humanity for his brutal treatment of rebels. He was found guilty in 2006.

The Insurgency

At first the Iraqi people, especially Shi'is and Kurds, were jubilant. They were thrilled by the end of Hussein's reign. But almost immediately, their happiness dissolved into anxiety. Although Iraq was filled with foreign troops, they did little to prevent the widespread looting and violence that broke out.

The invading force established the Coalition Provisional Authority to rule the country. It disbanded the Iraqi army and removed all members of the Ba'ath Party from government jobs. That decision meant that many Sunni Iraqis, accustomed to a privileged position, lost their jobs and status. Not surprisingly, many Sunnis became angry and violent. They and other frustrated Iraqis made up the insurgency that began to fight against the foreigners in their midst. Their fury was fueled by photographs of captured Iraqis being tortured by

Dan Senor (right), the spokesperson for the Coalition Provisional Authority, answers questions from journalists in 2004.

Jalal Talabani (shaking hands with soldier) was the first Kurdish president of Iraq. Talabani was a long-time supporter of Kurdish independence.

American troops in the Abu Ghraib prison. The photos were made public in 2004.

As Iraq was plunged into a civil war, ordinary Iraqis suffered horribly. Many were terrified to leave their homes because of the violence in the streets. Businesses closed, and people lost their jobs. Iraqis, impoverished and living in fear, struggled to find food or basic health care for their families. Many decided that if they were to survive, they had to leave their homeland. As many as two million people fled Iraq in the years following the 2003 invasion.

The United States formally handed over power to a temporary Iraqi government in June 2004. That government drafted a new constitution for the country and oversaw the election of 2005, which was largely boycotted by Sunni Iraqis. The new Iraqi government chose Nuri al-Maliki, a Shi'i, to be the country's prime minister and Jalal Talabani, a Kurd, to be its president.

In the years since, the violence has decreased, but it is far from over. A brutal attack in the city of Tikrit in March 2011 left about sixty people dead. There has also been a rise in assassinations of politicians and government officials.

At the same time, the United States is in the process of pulling combat troops out of Iraq. This is also causing tensions. Some Iraqis fear that the Iraqi army is not equipped to keep the peace by itself. Other Iraqis warn that if the United States does not pull its troops out, the insurgency will regroup and widespread violence will begin anew. Facing an uncertain future, the Iraqi people are once again left hoping for the best, while at the same time preparing for the worst.

As of 2011, there are still U.S. troops in Iraq.

Governing Iraq

On January 30, 2005, Iraqis from across the country traveled to polling stations to participate in their nation's first truly democratic election. After casting their votes, they were asked to dip a finger into a pool of purple ink. Marking voters with the ink was intended to prevent people from voting more than once. Many Iraqis displayed their purple fingers with pride. Holding their fingers in the air for all to see, they celebrated that at last they had a say in governing their country.

The election of 2005 was a thrilling moment for many Iraqis, who hoped that they could create a better, stronger, and fairer country. But building a new government from scratch was a difficult task for a number of reasons.

For one, the Iraqi people were deeply divided. Most felt far more loyalty to their religious and ethnic groups than they did to Iraq as a whole. In the new Iraq, three groups—Arab Sunnis, Arab Shi'is, and Kurds—would be vying for power.

Opposite: **An Iraqi woman displays her ink-stained finger, which shows that she voted in the 2005 elections.**

The Arab Sunni minority had been in control of Iraq during the previous regime. They were worried about losing power to the Shi'i Arabs, a group that included about 75 percent of the Iraqi people. The Kurds, an ethnic minority concentrated in the northeastern area of the country, had already established their own government, the Kurdistan Regional Government, even though officially their lands were still part of Iraq.

Sunni politician Tariq al-Hashimi became vice president following the 2005 elections.

The Kurdistan Regional Government

Since 1992, the three Iraqi governorates, or provinces, with the largest Kurdish population—Dohuk, Arbil, and Sulaymaniyah—have been ruled by the Kurdistan Regional Government. Its lawmaking body is the Iraqi Kurdistan Parliament, whose 111 members are elected by voters such as those pictured to the left. Citizens of the Kurdistan Region also vote for a president. This official shares power with the prime minister, who is chosen from the political party with the most seats in the parliament.

While Kurdistan is officially part of Iraq, in many ways it functions like a separate country. Its government issues its own passports and funds its own army. The Iraqi constitution of 2005 formally recognizes Kurdistan as a federal region with the right to self-government. It also names both Kurdish and Arabic as official languages of Iraq.

The Transitional National Assembly

Angry about losing power, many Sunnis refused to vote in the January 2005 election. Other Iraqis, however, came out in large numbers. About 60 percent of eligible voters made it to the polls.

These voters chose 275 representatives for the National Assembly of the Iraqi Transitional Government. This governing body was designed to be temporary. Its job was to draft a constitution—a set of written rules for how Iraq's new government would operate. The assembly was also supposed to prepare for another election, in which voters would select representatives to a permanent lawmaking body.

The Capital City

Baghdad, the capital of Iraq, has a long, proud history. It was founded in 762 by Abu Jafar al-Mansur, the caliph of the Abbasid Empire. During the eighth and ninth centuries, Baghdad emerged as the world's leading center for learning and scholarship. Before it was invaded by Mongols in 1258, the city was famed for its palaces, schools, and mosques (Islamic houses of worship).

Today, Baghdad is still one of the largest cities in the Middle East. Located on both banks of the Tigris River, it has an estimated population of 5,402,486. The section on the river's west bank is called Al Karkh, while the area on the east bank is known as Al Rasafa. Al Rasafa is the older and larger section of the capital.

Just a few decades ago, Baghdad was a modern city known for its sophistication. Funded by Iraq's oil industry, it was thriving as both a commercial and a cultural center. Its rapidly growing population enjoyed world-class museums, universities, and transportation systems. In recent years,

however, war and political unrest have taken an enormous toll on the city. Many of its buildings and bridges have been destroyed in bombing attacks, and the city struggles to provide adequate supplies of electricity and water to its residents. The people of Baghdad, however, look forward to the day they can rebuild their beloved city and restore it to its former glory.

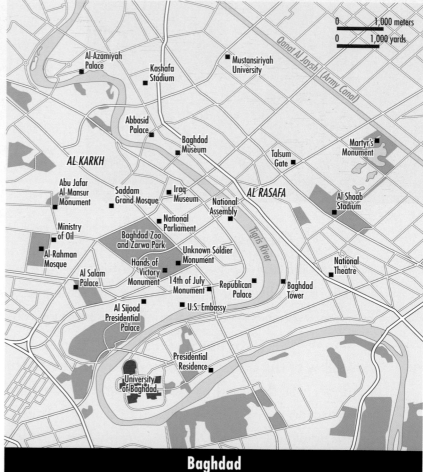

Baghdad

Before getting to work, the assembly members chose Jalal Talabani to serve as its president. Talabani was the first Kurd to serve in such a high position in any government in the modern Middle East. They also chose Shi'i leader Ibrahim al-Jaafari as the temporary Iraqi prime minister. In this post, al-Jaafari became the leader of the assembly.

A mosque lights up the night sky in Baghdad, the capital of Iraq.

Governing Iraq **59**

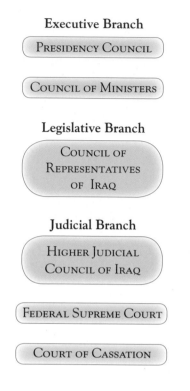

NATIONAL GOVERNMENT OF IRAQ

Executive Branch

PRESIDENCY COUNCIL

COUNCIL OF MINISTERS

Legislative Branch

COUNCIL OF
REPRESENTATIVES
OF IRAQ

Judicial Branch

HIGHER JUDICIAL
COUNCIL OF IRAQ

FEDERAL SUPREME COURT

COURT OF CASSATION

Three Branches of Government

By the fall of 2005, a committee of assembly members had produced a draft of the constitution. It established a government that, like those of the United States and Canada, was made up of three branches—legislative, executive, and judicial.

According to the constitution, the legislative, or lawmaking, branch is composed of two bodies—the Council of Representatives of Iraq (COR) and the Federation Council of Iraq. (As of 2011, Iraq had not yet established the Federation Council.) The COR is made up of 325 elected officials. Iraqis who are at least eighteen years old can vote for members of the COR.

The executive branch is headed by the Presidency Council. It includes a president and two vice presidents. The president is elected by the COR for no more than two four-year terms. The president signs all laws passed by the COR.

Members of the Council of Representatives raise their hands to vote.

The Flag of Kurdistan

The Kurdistan region of Iraq has its own official flag. The design features three bands—red on the top, white in the middle, and green on the bottom. In the center, overlapping all three bands is a gold-colored sun. The sun emblem has been associated with the Kurdish people since ancient times.

The Iraqi Flag

In 1963, when the Ba'ath Party first came to power, Iraq adopted a new flag. It featured three horizontal stripes—red, white, and black. On the white stripe in the middle were three green stars. The color combination appears on the flags of many other Arab countries, including Jordan, Kuwait, and the United Arab Emirates. Saddam Hussein in 1991 added the phrase "God is Great" in green Arabic script on the white stripe.

After the fall of Hussein, the U.S. occupying force wanted to do away with anything that reminded the Iraqis of their former dictator. With this goal in mind, the U.S.-appointed Iraqi Governing Council selected a new design for the national flag. It featured a blue crescent, representing Islam, on a field of white. At the bottom were two blue stripes (symbolizing the Tigris and Euphrates Rivers) separated by a yellow stripe (representing the Kurds).

The new design infuriated many Arab Iraqis. They were angry that the traditional colors of Arab people were wiped from the flag. Some also thought the flag looked too much like the blue-and-white flag of Israel, a nation toward which Iraq has been hostile.

Iraqi officials ended the controversy by immediately throwing out the new design. After holding a nationwide contest, the government came up with a temporary flag in 2008. This flag looks much like Iraq's earlier flag, except without the three stars.

The day-to-day responsibility for running the government, however, falls to the Council of Ministers of Iraq. Each minister is in charge of a certain area, such as agriculture, labor, education, environment, electricity, and culture. The Council of Ministers is headed by the prime minister, the most powerful position in the Iraqi government. The president nominates the prime minister from whatever political party has the most seats in the COR. The nominee then selects the other members of his Council of Ministers. However, the COR has to approve the prime minister and the proposed Council of Ministers before they can take their posts.

The judicial branch is made up of several courts. The Supreme Court is the highest court in the land. It has the

Supreme Court justices walk toward the Ministry of Justice Building in Baghdad after being sworn in.

Governorate Elections

Modern Iraq is divided into eighteen governorates, which are also called provinces. In addition to their representatives in the national government, Iraqi voters elect members of their governorate councils.

In 2009, fourteen governorates held council elections. For the first time since the war, candidates felt conditions were safe enough to actively campaign. All over Iraq, posters and banners announced the candidates' goals and visions for a peaceful and prosperous country. More than fourteen thousand people ran for only 444 council seats.

authority to make the final judgment on any case that comes before it. The Supreme Court also determines whether or not laws passed by the COR are in keeping with the constitution.

A man hangs a poster urging people to reject the new constitution.

Nuri al-Maliki

In April 2006, Nuri al-Maliki became the prime minister of Iraq's first permanent government after the fall of Saddam Hussein's regime. Maliki was born in 1950 in the village of Janajuh in the Babil governorate in central Iraq. He moved to Baghdad and attended the College of Usul al-Din, which was founded by a leader of the Da'wa political party. Soon after Maliki joined the Da'wa Party, the Ba'ath Party came to power in Iraq. The two parties considered each other enemies. When Saddam Hussein became president in 1979, he ordered the execution of all members of the Da'wa.

Maliki fled Iraq, living in other Middle Eastern countries for the next twenty-four years. All the while, he remained active in the Da'wa Party. While in exile, he helped found the Iraqi National Congress, which sought to end Saddam Hussein's rule.

After the fall of Baghdad in 2003, Maliki returned to his homeland. Less than two years later, he was elected to the Transitional National Assembly. This temporary assembly was charged with writing a new constitution for Iraq. Later in 2005, Maliki won a seat on the Council of Representatives, Iraq's new legislature. For months, the council struggled to select a prime minister who would be accept-able to all the major ethnic groups represented in it. Although not well known in Iraq, Maliki managed to win the post. He was appointed for a second term in late 2010, but only after a long political battle over who should lead Iraq.

As prime minister, Maliki has sometimes come into conflict with American officials. He has also had a tense relationship with the powerful Shi'i religious leader Muqtada al-Sadr, although it was only because of Sadr's support that Maliki received a second term.

Iraqis approved the new constitution on October 15, 2005. Two months later, they returned to the polls to elect the first Council of Representatives. Most Sunnis had boycotted the earlier election, but this time, they came out in large numbers. Even so, the majority of voters were again Shi'is. The Shi'i United Iraqi Alliance party won the most council seats, but no

The Iraqi legislature has 325 members.

political party held a majority. As a result, the various groups represented in the COR had trouble agreeing on who should be prime minister. After months of debate, the council finally chose Nuri al-Maliki, a little-known Shi'i politician. In April 2006, Maliki became the first prime minister of the new Iraqi government, while Jalal Talabani was named its president.

Ayad Allawi opposed the rule of Saddam Hussein and was forced to live outside Iraq for thirty years. He was able to return home after Hussein fell from power.

Muqtada al-Sadr is a fiery Shi'i religious leader who also has political influence.

Many Iraqis hoped that having the government in place would help end the violence. But the fighting continued, reaching its peak in 2007. Although conditions were improving as the next national election neared, many feared violence on election day. The election, originally scheduled in December 2009, was postponed until the following March. The turnout was heavy. Maliki's party, State of Law, won eighty-nine seats in the COR. But the Iraqi National Movement, led by Ayad Allawi, drew the support of both Shi'is and Sunnis and managed to take ninety-one seats.

Maliki challenged the results of the close election. Soon, Iraq's different political groups were accusing one another of trying to steal votes. For many months, they fought for control over the Council of Representatives. Eager to stay in power, Maliki won the support of many Kurdish politicians. He also courted Muqtada al-Sadr, an influential Shi'i religious leader. With Sadr's endorsement, Maliki emerged the victor. In December 2010, the Council of Representatives appointed him to his second term as Iraq's prime minister, with Talabani again serving as president.

To everyone hoping to see more stability in Iraq, the election of 2010 was unsettling. More than a year passed between the originally scheduled election day and the seating of the new government. But despite the tensions among the many political groups in Iraq, they were nevertheless able to compromise and settle their differences, at least for the moment. The election's confused aftermath was just one stumbling block out of many the Iraqis will likely encounter as they struggle to create a government that represents them all.

The National Anthem

When Saddam Hussein was in power, the official national anthem was "Ardulfurataini Watan," which means "the land of the two rivers." In 2004, Iraq adopted a new anthem. "Mawtini" ("My Homeland") is a folk song popular throughout the Arab world. Its lyrics were written in 1934 by Palestinian poet Ibrahim Touqan. The words celebrate the beauty of an unspecified homeland and vow victory over all its enemies.

My homeland, my homeland,
Glory and beauty, sublimity and splendor,
Are in your hills, are in your hills.
Life and deliverance, pleasure and hope
Are in your air, are in your air.
Will I see you, will I see you
Safe and comforted, sound and honored?
Will I see you in your eminence?
Reaching to the stars, reaching to the stars,
My homeland, my homeland.

Rebuilding the Economy

A S RECENTLY AS THE 1970S, THE ECONOMY OF Iraq was thriving. Its cities were growing at a rapid rate, drawing Iraqis from rural areas in search of good jobs and other opportunities. Much of this growth was fueled by the oil industry. Since the discovery of oil in Iraq in 1927, profits from oil production have accounted for most of the nation's wealth.

Sanctions and War

However, during the regime of Saddam Hussein, the economy of Iraq began to falter. After his army invaded Kuwait in 1990, the United Nations set out to punish him and erode his power. It imposed sanctions on Iraq. Because of the sanctions, many countries could not trade with Iraq. These sanctions mostly stayed in place until Hussein was overthrown in 2003.

Being cut off from international trade devastated the country. Iraq could no longer import much-needed goods from other countries. For many years, these forbidden imports included food and medicine. Hunger and illness, especially among children, became widespread. The sanctions also prevented the importation of chlorine, which is used to purify water. Large numbers of Iraqis became sick or died from a lack of clean water.

The sanctions were lifted in 2003, when Hussein was removed from power. But the invasion of Iraq caused new economic woes. Bombs destroyed much of the country's buildings, roads, and bridges. Iraq's electrical and sewage systems were also severely damaged.

The violence unleashed by the war made it even more difficult to get the Iraqi economy on firm footing. Insurgents staged hundreds of attacks on oil rigs and pipelines. The United States and its allies had promised to help rebuild Iraq, but much of the money they poured into the country was spent on extra security. The violence also scared off foreign investors, who might otherwise have lent support to Iraqi businesses.

Many buildings were damaged or destroyed in the recent war and its aftermath. Rebuilding will take a lot of time and money.

Money Facts

The basic unit of Iraqi currency is the dinar. In 2011, 1,166 dinars equaled US$1.00.

In 2003, Iraq issued a new series of paper money. For easy identification, the bills are printed in distinctive colors—purple for 50 dinars, light blue for 250 dinars, blue-green for 500 dinars, brown for 1,000 dinars, dark blue for 5,000 dinars, dark green for 10,000 dinars, and red for 25,000 dinars.

Illustrations on each bill celebrate some aspect of Iraqi life from the past or present. For instance, the front of the 500-dinar bill features the Dukan Dam, a modern engineering marvel that helps harness the water of the Little Zab River to produce hydroelectric power. The back shows an image of a carving of a winged bull with a human head. The carving was made about twenty-seven hundred years ago by an Assyrian artist in what is now Iraq.

The Oil Industry

Since 2008, the new Iraqi government has tried to revive the oil industry. The potential revenue from Iraqi oil is huge. The nation has the third-largest reserves of crude oil in the world.

By 2009, Iraq was producing about 2.4 million barrels of oil daily, making it the twelfth-largest oil producer in the world. It exports about 80 percent of that oil to other countries. The money these exports bring in make up more than 90 percent of the entire revenue of the Iraqi government.

In coming years, the oil industry in Iraq is likely to grow even more profitable. The government has signed contracts

An Iraqi farmer harvests barley. Iraq produces about 500,000 metric tons of barley each year.

with more than a dozen foreign oil companies. With their help, Iraq should be able to improve its oil infrastructure and its ability to reach the untapped reserves. Some experts suggest that one day Iraq will produce as much oil as Saudi Arabia, now the world's leading oil producer.

Farming and Livestock

Iraq is also working to revive its agricultural industry. About 22 percent of Iraqis work in agriculture. This includes most of the population that lives in rural areas.

In recent years, Iraq has had to import almost all the food it needs. But by using modern farming methods, it will likely be able to produce much more of the food that Iraqis eat. In addition to the rich lands of the Tigris and Euphrates Valleys, some drier areas can be transformed into good farmland through irrigation.

Iraq's most important agricultural products include wheat, barley, rice, and cotton. In the southern portion of the country, dates have long been harvested from large orchards of date palms.

Sheep, cattle, and goats are the most important livestock animals in Iraq.

In well-watered areas, many Iraqis also raise livestock, such as cattle, sheep, and goats. Most of the meat and milk from these animals is consumed by Iraqis. Their hides and wool, however, are often exported to neighboring countries.

Industry and Tourism

About one out of every five Iraqis works in industry. Many are involved in oil production. Others have jobs in manufacturing plants that make products such as chemicals, construction

What Iraq Grows, Makes, and Mines

Agriculture (2010)

Wheat	2,000,000 metric tons
Barley	1,150,000 metric tons
Rice	80,000 metric tons

Manufacturing (2008)

Fuel oil	107,128,000 barrels
Gasoline	17,228,000 barrels

Mining

Petroleum (2009)	2,400,000 barrels a day
Natural gas (2007)	1,422,000,000 cubic meters
Salt (2008)	109,000 metric tons

Large turbines inside Haditha Dam spin to generate power.

materials, processed foods, and cloth. Rich in natural gas, Iraq is also home to various power plants that create energy. Along its rivers are several hydroelectric plants, which use the power of flowing water to generate electricity.

Even more Iraqis work in service professions. In fact, about 60 percent are service workers. Many of them have jobs with the Iraqi government. Others work in the banking and retail industries.

While most of Iraq is still too dangerous to attract many foreign visitors, in the Kurdish northeast, tourism is flourishing. There, many Iraqis work in restaurants, clubs, and hotels. Kurdistan's cities also feature attractions such as amusement parks and golf courses.

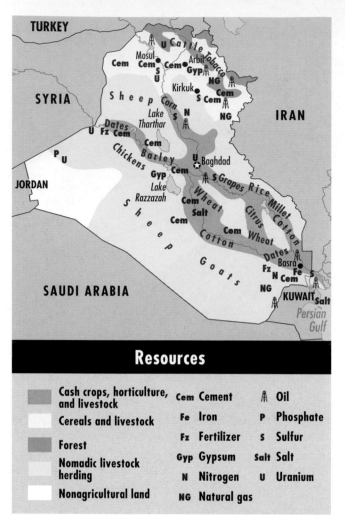

TURKEY

Mosul
Cem
Cem
Cem
Arbil
Gyp
Cattle
Tobacco
U
S
U
NG
Kirkuk
S
Cem
Cem
IRAN

SYRIA

Sheep
Corn
N
S
NG
Lake
Tharthar
U
Fz
Cem
Dates
Chickens
Barley
Cem
U
Baghdad
Cem
S Grapes Rice
Cem
Gyp
Lake
Razzazah
Cem
Wheat
Salt
Millet
Cotton
Cem
Citrus
Cem
Wheat
Cotton

JORDAN

P
U

Sheep
Goats
Dates
Fz
N
Basra
Fe
Cem
S
NG
KUWAIT Salt

SAUDI ARABIA

Persian Gulf

Resources

▨ Cash crops, horticulture, and livestock	**Cem** Cement	⚒ Oil
▢ Cereals and livestock	**Fe** Iron	**P** Phosphate
▨ Forest	**Fz** Fertilizer	**s** Sulfur
▢ Nomadic livestock herding	**Gyp** Gypsum	**Salt** Salt
▢ Nonagricultural land	**N** Nitrogen	**U** Uranium
	NG Natural gas	

Living conditions in Iraq have certainly improved in recent years. But the country still faces many economic challenges as it struggles to revive and rebuild its flagging industries. One continuing problem is unemployment. In 2009, about 15 percent of the working population could not find jobs. Many others could only find part-time or occasional work. As a result, about 25 percent of all Iraqis live in poverty. Many survive on food rations provided by the government.

Iraq still suffers from its broken infrastructure. Because of the destruction of roads and railways, getting around Iraq remains difficult. The opportunities to travel by air and train are still very limited and fairly expensive. Most people in cities rely on taxis, while in rural areas they generally get from place to place by using bicycles or animals.

Damage to phone lines has made business communication difficult. Iraqis, however, increasingly have access to mobile phones. A bigger problem is the lack of reliable electricity. By renovating electrical power plants and improving transmission lines, the country has dramatically increased the amount of electricity it generates. But the demand for electricity has grown even faster. With the sanctions lifted, Iraqi businesses and homes are now able to purchase computers, air conditioners, and other appliances. But with electrical blackouts common, Iraqis cannot rely on being able to use these items when needed.

Another obstacle to doing business in Iraq is the government. Only recently formed, it has not yet developed laws and policies needed to promote economic growth. But the government has been taking slow steps forward, particularly in its dealings with the oil industry. Especially with the promise of more income from oil, the economy and the standard of living of ordinary Iraqis seem poised to improve.

Iraqis fill out job applications on computers. With all the violence and destruction of recent years, finding a job can be difficult.

Arabs and Kurds

80

IRAQ IS HOME TO ABOUT THIRTY MILLION PEOPLE. By world standards, the Iraqi population is fairly young. About 40 percent of Iraqis are under the age of fifteen. Like many Middle Eastern countries, the Iraqi population is primarily Arab but also quite diverse. About three out of every four Iraqis belong to this ethnic group. Iraq also has a large Kurdish minority. About 15 percent of Iraqis identify themselves as Kurds. The rest of the population belongs to smaller minority ethnic groups. They include Turkmens, Armenians, and Assyrians.

Arabs and Kurds

Today, there are a total of about 300 million Arabs worldwide. Most live in western Asia and northern Africa. Approximately 22.5 million live in Iraq. Most Iraqi Arabs live in the central and southern portions of the country and in the northern city of Mosul.

Population of the Largest Cities (2010 est.)	
Baghdad	5,402,486
Mosul	2,882,442
Basra	1,914,205
Arbil	1,293,820
Kirkuk	864,351

For many centuries, Kurds have occupied the mountainous region in what is now eastern Turkey and Syria, western Iran, and northern Iraq. This area has long been called Kurdistan, meaning "land of the Kurds." Estimates vary, but the worldwide population of Kurds may be as high as twenty-five million.

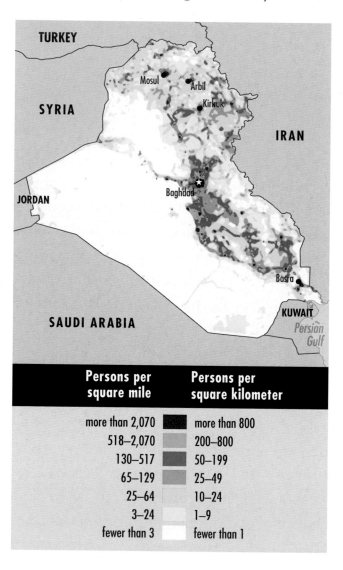

Persons per square mile		Persons per square kilometer
more than 2,070		more than 800
518–2,070		200–800
130–517		50–199
65–129		25–49
25–64		10–24
3–24		1–9
fewer than 3		fewer than 1

Ethnic Groups in Iraq

Arab	75 to 80%
Kurdish	15 to 20%
Turkmen, Assyrian, and other	5%

Many Kurds are farmers.

Traditionally, many Kurdish people were goatherds and sheepherders. But in the years following World War I (1914–1918), modern international borders divided up Kurdistan, disrupting the herders' abilities to travel from place to place. Today, most Kurds are city dwellers or farmers. They primarily belong to the Sunni sect of Islam, although some are Shi'is.

The Kurdish minority in Iraq has long sought independence. With Kurds in other nations, they hoped to establish a Kurdish state. Iraqi Kurds have historically endured brutal

Diverse Kirkuk

Tensions between Iraqi ethnic groups run high in the city of Kirkuk. Located in northern Iraq, it is home to a diverse population, including Kurds, Arabs, Turkmens, Armenians, and Assyrians.

The surrounding region is rich in oil. For many years, Iraq's government had a policy of "Arabization" toward Kirkuk. To keep the oil out of the hands of the Kurds, it expelled Kurds from the city and tried to increase its Arab population. Since the 2003 invasion, thousands of Kurds have returned to the region.

Today, the Kurds see Kirkuk as part of the Kurdish homeland and want to make it the capital of the Kurdish Regional Government. But the Arabs and other ethnic minorities there want the city and its oil wealth to remain under the control of the national government in Baghdad.

repression and discrimination. Life for the Kurds was especially difficult under Saddam Hussein. During his reign, many Kurds were killed, while others fled to Turkey and Iran.

Iraqi Kurds walk toward Iran. About 1.5 million Kurds fled Iraq after Saddam Hussein crushed an uprising in 1991.

Many Iraqis no longer live in their native land. These Iraqis fled the recent violence and took refuge in other countries. Although experts disagree on the exact number of refugees, probably about two million left Iraq after the 2003 invasion. The majority escaped to neighboring Syria and Jordan, but large numbers of Iraqi refugees also found their way to Iran, Turkey, Egypt, and Lebanon. Perhaps another two million Iraqis fled from their homes during the war and relocated somewhere else within Iraq.

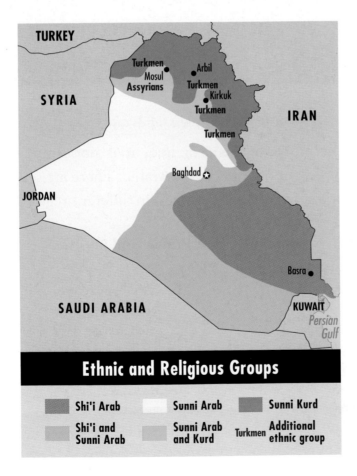

Ethnic and Religious Groups

- Shi'i Arab
- Sunni Arab
- Sunni Kurd
- Shi'i and Sunni Arab
- Sunni Arab and Kurd
- Turkmen — Additional ethnic group

Most Iraqis speak Arabic.

Languages of Iraq

Given the ethnic makeup of Iraq, it is not surprising that about 75 percent of Iraqis speak Arabic. There are several dialects (variations) of Arabic spoken in different regions of Iraq.

Common Arabic Words and Phrases	
al salaam alaykum	hello
ma' al-salama	good-bye
tisbah ala-khayr	good night (to a man)
tisbihin ala-khayr	good night (to a woman)
fursa sa'ida	pleased to meet you
Kif al-hal?	How are you?
Kif al-'a'ila?	How is your family?
baraka Allah bik	thank you
afwan	you're welcome

The Arabic Alphabet

The Arabic language is written down using the Arabic alphabet. Arabic is the second most-used alphabet in the world, following only the Latin alphabet, which is the one in which English and many other languages are written.

The Arabic alphabet is made up of twenty-eight letters. They are written and read from right to left. Today, Arabic is usually written in a cursive script based on the *naskhi* writing style. Calligraphers Ibn Muqlah and Siraj al-Shirazi are considered the originators of naskhi script.

But even if they speak different dialects, all Arabic-speaking Iraqis can generally understand one another.

Although most Iraqis speak Arabic, the government named both Arabic and Kurdish as official languages in the 2005 constitution of Iraq. One-fifth of Iraqis speak Kurdish. The Kurdish language is related to modern Persian, which is spoken in countries such as Iran and Afghanistan. Most Kurds of Iraq speak

Some road signs are in both Arabic and English.

In Iraq, children are required to attend school until age twelve. During and after the 2003 invasion, many schools were damaged or it was too dangerous to go outside, so attending school was not always possible.

one of two dialects, depending on where they are from. Kurds in the major Kurdish cities of Arbil and Sulaymaniyah speak the Sorani dialect. Residents of the Dohuk governorate use the Kurmanji dialect.

Kurds and other minorities often are bilingual—that is, they can speak two languages. Usually, they speak the language of their ethnic group and Arabic, which allows them to communicate with the majority of their countrymen. In urban areas, many Iraqis, especially businesspeople, are also bilingual. They generally speak English as well as their native Arabic or Kurdish. English is now taught in all Iraqi Kurdistan schools.

Minorities in Iraq speak a variety of other languages. For instance, the Turkmens who live around the northern cities of Kirkuk and Arbil speak Azeri Turkish. In the far south, along the border with Iran, a small number of Iraqis use the Persian language. Small Assyrian-speaking communities are found to the north, and Baghdad has pockets of Iraqis who use the Armenian language.

Before the most recent war, Iraq's literacy rate was on the rise. In 2000, an estimated 74 percent of Iraqis over age fifteen could read and write. Men had a higher rate than women—84 percent versus 64 percent—because they had greater access to education. As the new Iraqi government rebuilds its educational system, more Iraqis are likely to become literate, no matter what their native tongue.

Getting the News

No matter what language they speak, Iraqis have many ways to get the news of the day. Many people listen to news programs broadcast in Iraq and neighboring countries on the radio and, increasingly, on satellite television. During the common electrical blackouts, they can read one of the many newspapers available in Iraq. They include six daily papers—four in Arabic, one in Kurdish, and one in English. Far fewer Iraqis are able to make use of Internet news sources. In 2010, only about one in one hundred Iraqis had regular access to the Internet. Internet cafés, however, are becoming more popular, especially among the nation's young people.

A Muslim
Country

THE CONSTITUTION IRAQ ADOPTED IN 2005 DECLARES that "Islam is the official religion of the State." Islam is by far the most popular religion in the country. About 97 percent of Iraqis are Muslims. The other 3 percent observe a variety of religions, including Christianity, Judaism, and Yazidism. Although the Iraqi constitution "guarantees the Islamic identity of the majority of the Iraqi people," it grants people of other faiths religious freedom.

Opposite: **Mosques typically feature domes and tall towers called minarets.**

The Beginning of Islam

A traveling merchant named Muhammad first spread the news about Islam. He was born in Mecca, in what is now Saudi Arabia, around 570. Muslims believe that when Muhammad was about forty years old, the angel Gabriel began to appear to him. In these visitations, Gabriel communicated to Muhammad the word of God, which is "Allah" in Arabic.

Muhammad shared Gabriel's message with others in Mecca. At the time, his neighbors worshipped many gods. He told them to abandon these idols and embrace the one true

Religion in Iraq

Muslims	97%
Shi'i	60–65%
Sunni	32–37%
Others (includes Christians, Mandaeans, Yazidis, and Jews)	3%

All Muslims are supposed to make a pilgrimage to Mecca once in their life.

God. Muhammad also told them to live their lives in accordance with the revelations that Gabriel had shared with him.

Soon, Muhammad attracted followers interested in his new religion. They wrote down the messages he had received and compiled them into the Qur'an, the holy book of Islam. As the new religion grew, non-Muslim authorities worried that Muhammad was becoming too powerful. Muhammad and his followers were persecuted, so they left Mecca and moved north to the city of Medina in 622. This journey became known as the Hijra, and the year it occurred is treated as the year zero in the Muslim calendar. Throughout Muhammad's life, he attracted new converts to Islam. By his death in 632, most of the Arabs in the Arabian Peninsula were Muslim, although others continued to follow the Christian and Jewish faiths.

The Islamic Calendar

Iraqi Muslims determine when to celebrate religious holidays by consulting the Islamic calendar. The calendar is divided into twelve months, based on the phases of the moon. Each year is made up of 354 or 355 days, ten or eleven less than in the Western calendar, which is used in most of the world today. The Western calendar's dates for Islamic religious celebrations, therefore, change from year to year.

The Five Pillars of Islam

Today, Islam is the world's second-largest religion, after Christianity. There are more than 1.5 billion Muslims, including some 29 million in Iraq. Wherever they live, religious Muslims are supposed to practice religious duties known as the Five Pillars of Islam.

The first pillar, the *shahadah*, requires Muslims to affirm their faith with the words "There is no god but God, and Muhammad is the messenger of God." The second, *salah*, calls on Muslims to pray five times a day. The *zakat* commands them to give money to the poor or for social welfare. The *sawm* requires Muslims to fast during the month of Ramadan. The final pillar, *hajj*, obliges all Muslims, if they are able, to visit the holy city of Mecca at least once in their lives.

Devout Muslims observe several religious holidays. During Ramadan, the ninth month of the Islamic calendar,

When Muslims pray, they always face in the direction of Mecca.

The end of Ramadan is celebrated with joyous feasts.

Muslims fast during the daylight hours. They eat or drink only before the sun comes up and after it has gone down. During Ramadan, Muslims might make a special point of spending time reading the Qur'an or visiting their mosque.

When Ramadan comes to an end, Muslims celebrate 'Id al-Fitr. During this festive holiday, they visit and share meals with their friends and families. 'Id al-Adha is a more subdued religious observance. It commemorates when Ibrahim (known as Abraham in the Bible) expressed his willingness to sacrifice his son at God's command.

Sunnis and Shi'is

Although all Muslims share many religious beliefs, there are different groups within Islam. The division between Sunni Muslims and Shi'i Muslims has been especially important in the history of Iraq. The disagreements between the Sunnis and Shi'is date back to the death of Muhammad. The two groups had different ideas about who should be the Prophet's successor as the leader of all Muslims. The Sunnis held that the caliph should be selected from a group of elites. The Shi'is insisted that Muhammad had designated his cousin and son-in-law Ali Ibn Abi Talib as his successor, called an imam. Ali then selected his successor, Hasan, and so forth down the line of imams. Ali's supporters were called the Shi'at Ali (Party of Ali), which later gave the Shi'i branch of Islam its name.

Today, most of the Muslims in the world are Sunnis. The Shi'is are largely concentrated in Iran, southern Iraq and Kuwait, eastern Turkey, the Arabian Peninsula, and South Asia. Iraq is one of only five countries in which Shi'is are in the largest Muslim group (along with Iran, Azerbaijan, Bahrain, and Lebanon). About two-thirds of Iraq's Muslims are Shi'is.

In addition to their religious differences, Shi'is and Sunnis have held unequal status in Iraqi society. Under the rule of Saddam Hussein, the Sunnis had much more political power and many more economic opportunities. Not surprisingly, the Shi'i majority resented the Sunnis' elevated position. This ill will accounts for much of the violence between Iraqis in the country since 2003.

Shi'i Iraqis make their way to Karbala. This pilgrimage was banned under Saddam Hussein's rule.

A Shi'i Shrine

Najaf, in central Iraq, is one of the holiest cities for Shi'i Muslims. According to Muslim tradition, the biblical figure Abraham once visited the area where Najaf now stands. Abraham supposedly said that anyone buried there would spend eternity in paradise.

In 661, Ali Ibn Abi Talib, the son-in-law and cousin of Muhammad revered by the Shi'is, was assassinated. He was buried in Najaf, where his shrine is still visited by Shi'i pilgrims. The city also houses the Wadi al-Salam, or Valley of Peace. It is one of the largest cemeteries in the world.

Other Religions

Three percent of the people in Iraq belong to religions other than Islam. One is Yazidism, which contains beliefs and practices that resemble those of Islam, Christianity, Judaism, and Zoroastrianism (a religion that originated in Iran during the sixth century). The majority of Yazidis in the world live in Iraqi Kurdistan. The Yazidis believe that there is one true God, who is assisted by seven angels. The most important is Melek Taus, or the Peacock Angel. In Iraq, the Yazidis have long been a persecuted minority. One particularly horrific instance of violence occurred in August 2007 in the village of Qahtaniya, where suicide bombers killed more than five hundred Yazidi Kurds.

Christianity is believed to have been first introduced to Iraq in the first century CE. The exact number of Christians in Iraq is not known, but as many as 50 percent of Christian

Muqtada al-Sadr

Muqtada al-Sadr, a Shi'i religious leader, is an outspoken critic of the American invasion and occupation of Iraq. He has been very involved in the creation of the new Iraqi government following the fall of Saddam Hussein.

Born around 1974, he is the son of Mohammed Sadiq al-Sadr, one the most respected Shi'i religious figures. In 1999, his father and two of his brothers were murdered, probably by officials in Hussein's government.

Sadr grew in prominence after the U.S.-led invasion of Iraq in 2003. He publicly demanded that all coalition troops leave the country. Sadr received especially strong support from the residents of Sadr City, a poor area in Baghdad named after his father. Some of his supporters joined the Mahdi Army, which engaged the coalition forces in armed combat.

In the 2010 elections, Sadr encouraged his followers to vote. Their showing at the polls gave him considerable power in the new government, even though he held no elected position. Although he had previously had a falling-out with Shi'i politician Nuri al-Maliki, Sadr decided to support him for prime minister.

By 2011, Sadr was being particularly vocal about his support of the total withdrawal of American troops from Iraq by the end of that year. He suggested that if the U.S. soldiers did not leave, he would command the feared Mahdi Army to return to the battlefield.

Catholics sing at a Christmas mass in Baghdad. An estimated three hundred thousand Catholics live in Iraq.

Iraqis are thought to have fled the country after 2003. Facing hostility from the Muslim majority in Iraq, many escaped into Syria, Jordan, and Lebanon. Some Christians who did not leave Iraq relocated to Kurdistan, where they felt safer. Reportedly, some Baghdad Christians moved to new neighborhoods in the city where they could more easily hide their faith or protect themselves from persecution.

Other religious groups found in Iraq include Mandaeans and Jews. The Mandaeans belong to a very old religion. They believe that John the Baptist was the Messiah, or savior of humankind. At one time, there was a large, flourishing Jewish community in Iraq, especially in Baghdad. When the Jewish state of Israel was created in 1948, however, many Iraqi Jews, facing growing persecution in their homeland, decided to move to that country. Today, there are probably fewer than one hundred Jews in Iraq.

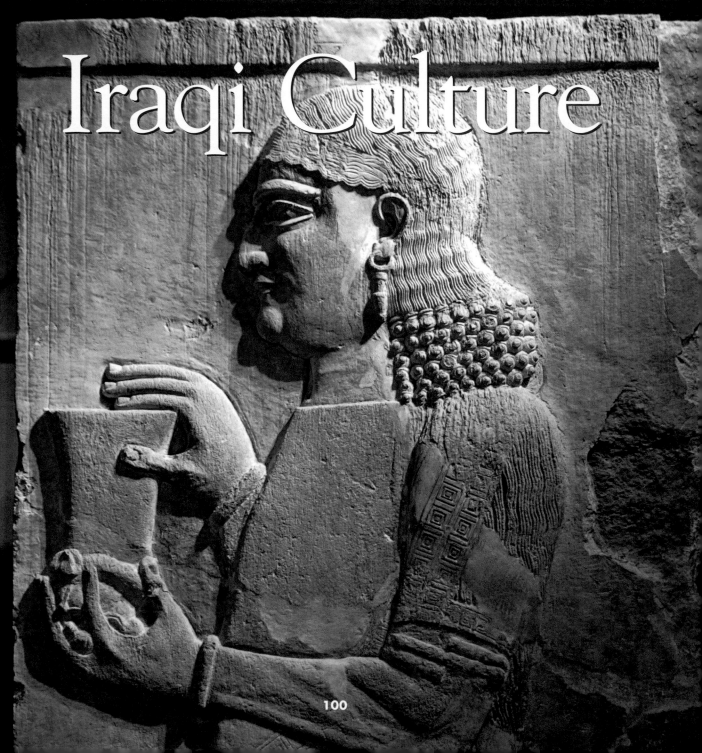

Iraqi Culture

F OR MANY DECADES IN IRAQ, THE ARTS HAVE BEEN strongly linked to politics. When Saddam Hussein was in power, he saw art as a tool for propaganda—that is, for promoting a certain political point of view. During his rule, writers, poets, painters, playwrights, and filmmakers did not feel free to create the type of art they wanted to make. Instead, they were pressured by Hussein's regime to make works that celebrated and glorified the dictator and his government. Many artists refused to participate in his scheme. They either stopped making art or left the country so they could work without fear of government interference or intimidation.

Unfortunately, when Hussein lost power, conditions for Iraqi artists grew even worse. Like other Iraqis, they struggled just to survive in the chaos and violence unleashed by the invasion of Iraq in 2003. In addition, most of the institutions that promoted and supported the arts in Iraq were damaged or destroyed. As looters and gangs roamed Iraq's streets, they often took out their anger on government-funded arts

Opposite: **The National Museum of Iraq displays artifacts from the nation's remarkable past.**

An official from the National Museum of Iraq mourns the damage done to the priceless objects there. Many artifacts were stolen or damaged during the chaos of 2003.

organizations. Thieves broke into Baghdad's Institute of Fine Arts, stole musical instruments, and destroyed its grand piano.

Most alarming of all was the looting of the National Museum of Iraq. People around the world were horrified by newscasts showing looters raiding the museum and making off with its treasures—many beautiful and priceless artifacts from the oldest civilizations on earth. In all, about fifteen thousand items were stolen. Although some artifacts have been returned to Iraq, most are still lost, possibly forever.

Since that time, Iraqi artists have worked to rebuild their nation's creative community. Through these efforts and through their art, they are trying to help themselves and others come to terms with their country's difficult history.

Literature and the Visual Arts

Much of Iraq's contemporary literature is a mix of old and new artistic traditions. Given that people of the region have loved poetry for thousands of years, it is not surprising that many of Iraq's leading modern literary figures are poets. One of the best known is Badr Shakir Al-Sayyab, whose book of poems titled *Song of Rain* (1960) is considered a classic in Arabic literature. Another of Iraq's greatest poets is Nazik al-Malaika. She was famous for being the first prominent Arabic poet to write in the modern form of free verse.

Many of Iraq's major visual artists of recent decades trained or taught at the Institute of Fine Arts in Baghdad. They included painters Ismail Fatah Al Turk and Layla

Ismail Fatah Al Turk was best known for designing the Martyr's Monument, a memorial to the Iraqis who died in 2004 in the Iran-Iraq War. The monument's split dome rises 130 feet (40 m) high.

Al-Attar and sculptor Jawad Saleem. The institute has long been a haven for Iraqi artists, but recently it has come under attack. Bowing to pressure by religious groups, the Ministry of Education in 2010 banned all theater and music classes there, prompting an angry outcry from its students. The Ministry of Culture, on the other hand, has worked to preserve knowledge of traditional Iraqi crafts, such as carpet making and copper working.

Music in Iraq

The music scene in Iraq is a mixture of old and new, with traditional Arabic music heard alongside contemporary musical styles. One of the most popular traditional styles of music there is *maqam*. Maqam had its origins in ancient times. But in the decades after Iraq's founding, the musical style became closely associated with the country's new national identity.

Filming Today's Iraq

Iraq's film industry is small but growing. The best-known Iraqi filmmaker is Mohamed Al-Daradji. He filmed his 2006 drama, *Ahlaam* (*Dreams*), during some of the worst violence of the Iraq War. It tells the story of two patients who escape from a psychiatric hospital into the streets of the war-torn capital. His second feature, *Son of Babylon* (2010), follows a boy and his grandmother as they search for a long-lost relative after the 2003 invasion. It was Iraq's submission for the 2011 Academy Award for Best Foreign Language Film.

Ilham al-Madfai combines Western guitar playing with traditional Iraqi music.

In the maqam style, performers sing lyrics based on old Arabic poems. They are usually accompanied by musicians playing traditional instruments. These include the oud, a stringed instrument similar to a lute, and the *santur*, a type of dulcimer.

Modern styles embraced by Iraqi music lovers include rock, pop, and rap. One favorite Iraqi musician is Ilham al-Madfai. Nicknamed the Baghdad Beatle, al-Madfai helped popularize the guitar in Iraq and formed the country's first rock band. Another favorite is Iraqi-Moroccan performer Shada Hassoun. Now one of the most popular singers in the Middle East, she rose to stardom after winning the television talent contest *Star Academy Arab World* in 2007. She was the first woman to be in the competition, and she memorably held out an Iraqi flag with pride when she was announced the winner.

International Pop Star

For more than two decades, Kadim al-Sahir has been one of the most famous and beloved Iraqi entertainers. Born in 1961, al-Sahir was raised in Baghdad. As a young teenager, he began playing the guitar and took up singing in the classic Iraqi maqam style. After studying music in Baghdad, al-Sahir broke into the record business with a hit single, "Ladghat el Hayya" ("The Snake Bite"), which was censored by the Iraqi government. Al-Sahir became known for his movie-star good looks and his romantic ballads, which combined elements of traditional Iraqi songs and modern pop styles.

After surviving the bombing of Baghdad during the 1991 Persian Gulf War, al-Sahir left Iraq. He eventually settled in Cairo, Egypt, and began to attract an international audience. He was especially popular among Iraqis who, like him, had moved away from his war-torn native land. They particularly loved his song "Kathura Al Hadeeth" ("Beauty and Love"). It tells the story of a man whose girlfriend suspects he has another love. The song's end reveals that his second love is not a woman, but the city of Baghdad.

In 2003, just before the U.S-led invasion of Iraq, al-Sahir began a tour of the United States. He told the *Detroit Free Press* that he hoped the tour would help Americans see Iraqis in a positive light. "[Iraqis are] artists, philosophers, poets, they're singers, writers," he explained. "They're a creative people, a peace-loving people."

Across Iraq, people enjoy classical music performed by the Iraqi National Symphony Orchestra. The orchestra, founded in 1959, was left in disarray by the 2003 invasion. During the aftermath, it struggled to find funding, and many of its musicians fled the country to escape the violence. Since then, chief conductor Karim Wasfi, with the financial support of the Ministry of Culture, has slowly rebuilt the orchestra. In 2011, it employed ninety musicians from a variety of ethnic groups and religious backgrounds. When it is not playing to packed houses in its permanent home at the Institute of Fine Arts in Baghdad, it tours the nation giving free concerts. Wasfi proudly told the *Wall Street Journal*, "I'm now able to struggle with artistic quality—getting the music right—rather than logistics or mere survival."

Karim Wasfi leads the Iraqi National Symphony Orchestra.

Ballet is a popular activity among young Iraqis.

For young people interested in performing music, the national orchestra established an after-school music academy. Other music students attend the Baghdad School of Music and Ballet. Established in the late 1960s, it offers students academic courses and instruction in ballet and in playing instruments, both modern and traditional. Since 2007, another program available for young people is a summer camp in Arbil sponsored by the Kurdistan Regional Government and the U.S. Embassy. With the help of the nonprofit organization American Voices, the camp brings in American artists to train young Iraqis in a wide range of performing styles—from classical music to jazz to hip-hop. In 2010, a concert featuring the program's three hundred graduates was aired on national television in Iraq.

Finding Humor in Hard Times

Under Saddam Hussein's rule, Iraqis had to be careful about what they said. If they were heard criticizing the government, they could face harsh punishment or even death. After Hussein fell from power, Iraqi comedians had the chance to express their dry and sometimes dark sense of humor. One of the most popular Iraqi television shows during the post-war era was *Caricatures*. It featured comedy sketches that made fun of everyday life in Iraq. In 2004, one of the program's stars, Walid Hassan, explained, "We laugh because we are done crying." To the despair of his fans, Hassan was shot and killed while driving through Baghdad in 2006.

An Iraqi soccer player (in white) fights for the ball with a player from Singapore during a match in 2011.

Soccer and Basketball

Even with all their divisions and differences, most people of Iraq do have one thing in common—their love of soccer. Before the rule of Saddam Hussein, the Iraqi national team was a powerhouse in international competitions in the Middle East. But under Hussein, because of UN sanctions, the team was banned from competing against other national teams. The team was also placed under the control of Hussein's son Uday, who tortured players who did not perform to his expectations.

Basketball is growing in popularity in Iraq.

Since that dark time, the country has worked to rebuild its national team. It had its greatest victory in 2007, when it beat the Saudi Arabian team to win the Asian Football Confederation Asian Cup tournament. In a rare moment of national unity, Iraqi fans of all backgrounds came together to celebrate. In addition to cheering on the national team, Iraqis also enjoy attending contests between the twenty-eight local teams that make up the Iraqi Premier League.

In Iraq, the second most-beloved sport is basketball. The Iraqi Basketball Association organizes leagues for adults and young people across the country. Iraq's best players make up its sixteen professional teams, whose season ends in a championship game.

Until recently, Iraq had two major sports centers—the Al Shaab National Stadium in Baghdad and Franso Hariri Stadium in Arbil. But in the city of Basra, the Iraq government funded the construction of the biggest sports complex ever built in Iraq. Basra Sports City features two stadiums, including one with sixty-five thousand seats, and four hotels. It is slated to host the 2013 Gulf Cup of Nations, an international soccer competition played by teams representing eight countries in the Middle East.

Olympic Athlete

When Dana Hussein Abdul-Razzaq was growing up, being an athlete in Iraq was dangerous business. Uday Hussein, son of dictator Saddam Hussein, was known to torture Iraqis if they failed to win sporting competitions. Understandably, Abdul-Razzaq's parents did everything they could to keep her away from sports.

With the fall of Saddam Hussein in 2003, the seventeen-year-old saw an opportunity. She began running track, even as the violence between Shi'is and Sunnis grew by the day. A Shi'i athlete training with a Sunni coach, Abdul-Razzaq kept her sights on the Olympics, despite the fact that it was hard for her to even find a decent pair of running shoes in her war-torn country.

Abdul-Razzaq succeeded in capturing a place on the seven-member Iraqi Olympic team. She was to be the only female athlete representing Iraq at the 2008 Summer Olympics in Beijing, China. However, just months before the Olympics, the International Olympic Committee banned Iraq from participating because of political infighting between the Iraqi government and the nation's Olympic organizers.

Eventually, the ban was lifted in time for Abdul-Razzaq to compete in Beijing. She ran the 100-meter sprint in 12.13 seconds, but her time was not good enough for her to advance in the competition. Although she did not win an Olympic medal, she overcame enormous obstacles to represent her people and, in her eyes, help bring them closer together. As she explained to *Time* magazine, "Sports can unify the Iraqi people—no Sunnis, no Shi'is, just sport for the country."

Preserving Iraqi Culture

As Iraq changes, so does its cultural life. Young writers, artists, musicians, and sports stars are all helping to redefine how Iraqis think of themselves and their country. But the Iraqis are also conscious of their renowned past and are eager to preserve it for future generations.

One important program with that goal is the Iraq Cultural Heritage Project. Funded by the U.S. Embassy, the project has helped establish the Iraqi Institute for the Conservation of Antiquities and Heritage in Arbil. The institute trains Iraqis to be museum professionals so they can record and preserve Iraq's cultural treasures.

Samir Sumaida'ie, the Iraqi ambassador to the United States, announces the launch of the Iraq Cultural Heritage Project in 2008.

The project also provided funds to repair and modernize Iraq's looted National Museum. With these funds and grants from other countries, the museum has refurbished its exhibit halls, improved its storage space, and installed air-conditioning.

In 2011, the Iraqi government announced that the National Museum, once the pride of Baghdad, would be opened to the general public. Anyone with an Internet connection can view highlights from its collection online at the Virtual Museum of Iraq (www.virtualmuseumiraq.cnr.it /homeENG.htm), a project funded by the Italian Ministry of Foreign Affairs. The online gallery allows people around the world to learn about the glorious art and artifacts of ancient Iraq.

Prime Minister Nuri al-Maliki (center) and other Iraqi officials tour the National Museum of Iraq.

CHAPTER TEN

Everyday Challenges

114

I N MANY WAYS, LIVING CONDITIONS IN IRAQ HAVE improved since the violent years following the 2003 invasion. But the war and its aftermath continue to loom large as the Iraqi people try to rebuild their nation and their lives.

Opposite: **On average, Iraqis attend school for ten years.**

Family Life

The lives of most Iraqis revolve around their extended families. Family bonds are traditionally tight. But the nation's recent troubles have made these ties even more important as family members rely heavily on one another to endure daily struggles.

Status in the family is mostly determined by age and gender. Older men hold the highest status. Their wives and children are expected to at least appear to respect and obey them. Iraq's laws reinforce this power structure. But the reality within families is far more complex. In some families, a woman who has a strong will, personality, or political skills may be the real decision maker in the family.

When children grow up, their parents are usually involved in the process of choosing who they will marry. Parents frequently arrange marriages with relatives. In fact, as many as half of all marriages in Iraq are between first or second cousins. Weddings are large, festive events, sometimes with hundreds of people in attendance.

Many Iraqi women are housewives, but some work outside the home. Women hold important jobs in a wide variety of fields, including government, business, and media. At social gatherings, however, men and women tend to remain in separate groups. Any public physical display of affection between a woman and a man is frowned upon.

After the 2003 invasion of Iraq, some Muslim religious leaders began pushing for stricter social controls of

Many Iraqi women work in business. This woman is writing on a board at the Iraq Stock Exchange.

When an Iraqi couple gets married, they hold a series of parties. The last one is the Sab'a, which means "seven" in Arabic. Traditionally, the Sab'a was scheduled seven days after the wedding. Today, it is usually held whenever the couple returns from their honeymoon. The party is held at the home of the groom's family, but he isn't invited. Only women get to attend a Sab'a. They bring gifts for the bride to help her and her husband set up their new home.

women. Because of that pressure and the dramatic rise in violence all over Iraq, some women stopped working outside the home. Many also changed their style of dress. As Iraqis grew more angry at the American occupying force, many rejected the Western-style clothing that had been commonplace in Iraq, especially in its cities. To avoid harassment, some women started wearing more traditional clothing, including the *hijab* (a headscarf) and the *abaya* (a black cloak that leaves only the eyes and hands uncovered).

Eating in Iraq

Iraqi food is similar to that eaten in other Middle Eastern countries. Many meals feature yogurt, rice, beans, bread, and fresh vegetables and fruits, particularly dates. Meat, especially lamb and fish, are enjoyed by Iraqis who can afford it. Tea is the most popular drink. Dishes commonly featured in Iraqi meals include *shawarma* (shaved meat and vegetables in a

Fish is cooked over an open flame to make masgouf.

pita), falafel (fried chickpea patties), and *quzi* (grilled lamb stuffed with rice, spices, nuts, and raisins).

When asked to name their favorite meal, many Iraqis will say *masgouf*. The dish consists of a whole fish, most commonly a carp. The fish is sliced open, stuffed with spices, and skewered. It is then cooked slowly on an open fire. Often served with vegetables and bread, the fish has a sweet and smoky flavor. Masgouf is usually served only on special occasions. Restaurants all over Iraq pride themselves on their own unique takes on this national dish.

Tabbouleh

Like many other people across the Middle East, Iraqis enjoy a refreshing salad called tabbouleh. A mixture of bulgur wheat, parsley, mint, and other ingredients, tabbouleh gets its bite from a dressing of lemon juice and olive oil.

Ingredients

½ cup bulgur wheat

1 cup parsley, chopped

½ cup mint, chopped

1 cup grape tomatoes, halved

3 tablespoons olive oil

2 tablespoons lemon juice

Salt and pepper, to taste

1 bunch scallions, chopped

Directions

Prepare the bulgur wheat according to package instructions. In a large bowl, mix the cooked wheat with all the other ingredients. Enjoy!

Iraqis enjoy sharing food with friends and visitors. Being invited to a family's home for dinner is considered an honor. Known for their hospitality, Iraqi hosts work hard to offer the finest food possible and to make sure their guests leave contented and well fed.

Rural and Urban

The everyday life of Iraqis varies considerably depending on where they live. The biggest divide is between rural and urban life. About one-third of Iraqis live in rural areas. Most live in small villages, where community life centers on the market or the local mosque. Their rectangular houses are made of dried mud and brick. Generally, rural Iraqis make their living off the land. Most of them farm small plots or raise livestock.

Girls walk through a village in southeastern Iraq.

The majority of Iraqis live in urban areas. Baghdad, Basra, and other major Iraqi cities are full of modern buildings and crowded roads. For Iraqis living in cities, life is faster paced. City life also brings them into contact with more people of varied backgrounds.

Because of the country's ongoing security problems, urban dwellers in Iraq do not get to take advantage of many of the pleasures of city life. There are still some restaurants, cafés, theaters, and museums where people can gather. But many businesses and cultural institutions have closed either temporarily or permanently.

The one area where city life is as active as ever is Iraqi Kurdistan. With relatively little violence and a healthy economy, cities such as Arbil and Sulaymaniyah are growing

People in the city of Arbil enjoy a trip to the bowling alley.

fast. Throughout these cities, there is a construction boom. Residents and tourists flock to their rising skyscrapers, restaurants, and shiny new shopping malls.

Surviving Shortages

The prosperity found in Iraqi Kurdistan, however, is more the exception than the rule. Although violence has decreased, Iraq is still an unstable country with a crippled economy. Many people continue to face extraordinary challenges just to survive from day to day.

One of the biggest problems people have is getting food. Food prices are high in Iraq, especially for the unemployed.

Kurdish cities such as Arbil are booming. This hotel opened in 2011.

About 60 percent of the population relies on food rations provided by the government. Even though much of the government's budget goes to funding the rations, the food is often of low quality, and sometimes the rations are too small to keep people from going hungry.

Another problem Iraqis still face is a lack of electricity. The new government has greatly increased the amount of electricity generated in the country, but it falls far short of the amount that is needed. The demand for electricity is growing fast because, with the UN sanctions no longer in place, Iraqis can now buy many small appliances, including computers, for the first time. The national power grid supplies electricity for only one out of every five hours, so for much of the day, many Iraqis have no electricity. Power shortages are especially severe in the summer, when air-conditioning use increases.

Water is also in short supply. In the best of times, Iraq lacks sufficient water for drinking and irrigation. But in recent years, reduced levels of rainfall have created a water crisis. The situation is particularly bad in Kirkuk, where competition for dwindling water supplies has increased ethnic tensions.

Many Iraqis suffer from a lack of access to health care. Medical supplies are scarce in the country—a particularly

Many parts of Iraq suffer water shortages. These boys are carrying water to their village from an irrigation canal.

A professor gives lessons to medical students at Karbala University. Iraq currently has a shortage of doctors.

difficult situation for the many people suffering from wartime injuries. Hospitals often do not have enough doctors and nurses to care for their patients.

Back to School

Another major concern is the condition of Iraq's schools. Its public school system was once one of the best in the Middle East. But under Saddam Hussein, funding for education was slashed by 90 percent. With the UN sanctions and war, fewer and fewer young people were able to attend school. As a result, the country's literacy rate dropped substantially.

The Iraqi government estimates that the country needs about fifty-eight hundred new school buildings. Rural areas are especially in need of schools. In addition, old school buildings have to be repaired and improved. Many were damaged and looted after the 2003 invasion. Others are tents or makeshift structures thrown together from mud and straw. Only 30 percent of Iraq's school buildings provide access to clean water and toilets.

Getting girls back in school is a high priority for the Ministry of Education. Like most Middle Eastern countries, girls and young women once made up nearly half of Iraq's students. But after the invasion, many parents insisted their daughters drop out. Because of the level of violence on the streets, some families barely let their girls leave the house.

Into the Future

In the spring of 2011, people in many Middle Eastern countries took to the streets and protested, demanding sweeping changes in their governments. Tunisia, Egypt, Libya, Bahrain, Yemen, and Syria were just a few of the countries that saw such protests during what became known as the Arab Spring movement.

Al Mahibs

At night during Ramadan, young Iraqis love to play a game called Al Mahibs. The players divide into two teams. One player on each team holds a ring. Each team tries to guess who on the other side has the ring. Whichever team guesses correctly wins. Often, the losing players are expected to provide the winners with sweets and soft drinks. Sharing these treats, all players enjoy a feeling of togetherness. In recent years, Baghdad officials have encouraged teams from Shi'i and Sunni neighborhoods to play against one another in the hope of healing old wounds.

Many people took to the streets of Baghdad in 2011 to demand better services.

Some protests were held in Iraq, but for the most part, the Iraqi protesters were not seeking an entirely new government. They instead called for improved water supplies, increased food rations, and reliable electricity—in essence, better services from the government they had so painstakingly just put together. The protests reflected the cautious optimism that many Iraqis now feel about their country. Rather than feeling the need to start over, they desperately want to take the nation they have now and improve it. After so much hardship, they continue to believe that Iraq has a chance to emerge as a stable and prosperous nation.

The problems Iraq faces are many—ethnic strife, religious division, economic chaos, crumbling infrastructure, and more. But Iraq does have one important resource: the third-largest supply of oil in the world. If its social and political climate calms and the country can more successfully tap into its oil supply, life in Iraq is likely to change rapidly and for the better.

But Iraq has a second resource just as valuable—the extraordinary resilience of the Iraqi people. They have seen many horrors in recent years, yet they remain proud, determined, and ready to move forward toward a brighter day.

Iraqi National Holidays

New Year's Day	January 1
Army Day	January 6
Baghdad Liberation Day	April 9
Food and Agriculture Organization Day	April 17
Labor Day	May 1
Republic Day	July 14
Cease-fire Day	August 8
Iraqi Independence Day	October 3

Many holidays in Iraq are based on the Islamic calendar. Because this calendar is shorter than the Western calendar, the dates on which these holidays fall in the Western calendar change from year to year. These holidays include:

Mouloud

'Id al-Fitr

'Id al-Adha

Islamic New Year

Ashura

Timeline

	Iraqi History			World History
Sumerian civilization develops in present-day Iraq.	**ca. 4000** BCE		**ca. 2500** BCE	Egyptians build the pyramids and the Sphinx in Giza.
Babylonian ruler Nebuchadnezzar II builds the Hanging Gardens of Babylon.	**ca. 600** BCE		**ca. 563** BCE	The Buddha is born in India.
			313 CE	The Roman emperor Constantine legalizes Christianity.
Arab Muslims take control of what is now Iraq.	638 CE		610	The Prophet Muhammad begins preaching a new religion called Islam.
The Prophet Muhammad's grandson, al-Husayn ibn Ali, is killed at the Battle of Karbala.	680			
Baghdad is founded as the capital of the Abbasid Empire.	762			
			1054	The Eastern (Orthodox) and Western (Roman Catholic) Churches break apart.
			1095	The Crusades begin.
			1215	King John seals the Magna Carta.
A Mongol army invades and destroys Baghdad.	1258		1300s	The Renaissance begins in Italy.
			1347	The plague sweeps through Europe.
			1453	Ottoman Turks capture Constantinople, conquering the Byzantine Empire.
			1492	Columbus arrives in North America.
Iraq becomes part of the Ottoman Empire.	1533		1500s	Reformers break away from the Catholic Church, and Protestantism is born.
			1776	The U.S. Declaration of Independence is signed.
			1789	The French Revolution begins.

Iraqi History

The League of Nations gives Great Britain control over Iraq.	1920
Oil is discovered near the Iraqi city of Kirkuk.	1927
The modern nation of Iraq is founded.	1932
Iraq becomes a republic after a military coup overthrows the Iraqi monarchy.	1958
The Ba'ath Party takes control of Iraq.	1968
Saddam Hussein becomes Iraq's president.	1979
The Iran-Iraq War is fought.	1980–1988
The United Nations places economic sanctions on Iraq after Iraq invades Kuwait.	1990
A U.S.-led coalition of troops drives the Iraqi army from Kuwait during the Persian Gulf War.	1991
A U.S.-led coalition force ousts Saddam Hussein from power.	2003
Insurgents battle coalition forces.	2004
Iraqi voters approve a new national constitution and elect the first permanent postwar government.	2005

World History

1865	The American Civil War ends.
1879	The first practical lightbulb is invented.
1914	World War I begins.
1917	The Bolshevik Revolution brings communism to Russia.
1929	A worldwide economic depression begins.
1939	World War II begins.
1945	World War II ends.
1957	The Vietnam War begins.
1969	Humans land on the Moon.
1975	The Vietnam War ends.
1989	The Berlin Wall is torn down as communism crumbles in Eastern Europe.
1991	The Soviet Union breaks into separate states.
2001	Terrorists attack the World Trade Center in New York City and the Pentagon near Washington, D.C.
2004	A tsunami in the Indian Ocean destroys coastlines in Africa, India, and Southeast Asia.
2008	The United States elects its first African American president.

Fast Facts

Official name: Republic of Iraq

Capital: Baghdad

Official languages: Arabic and Kurdish

Baghdad

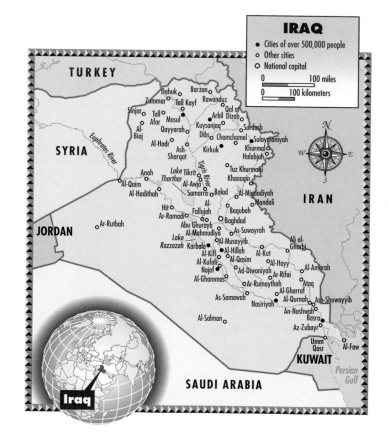

Iraqi flag

Euphrates River

Official religion:	Islam
Year of founding:	1932
National anthem:	"Mawtini" ("My Homeland")
Government:	Parliamentary democracy
Chief of state:	President
Head of government:	Prime minister
Area:	169,235 square miles (438,317 sq km)
Latitude and longitude of geographic center:	33° N, 44° E
Bordering countries:	Turkey to the north; Syria, Jordan, and Saudi Arabia to the west; Kuwait to the south; and Iran to the east
Highest elevation:	Cheekha Dar, 11,847 feet (3,611 m) above sea level
Lowest elevation:	Persian Gulf, sea level
Highest average temperature:	111°F (44°C) in August
Lowest average temperature:	39°F (4°C) in January
Highest annual rainfall:	Mountainous region, 2 feet (0.6 m)
Lowest annual rainfall:	Desert, 4 inches (10 cm)

Shrine of Ali Ibn Abi Talib

National population (July 2011 est.): 30,399,572

Population of major cities (2010 est.):

Baghdad	5,402,486
Mosul	2,882,442
Basra	1,914,205
Arbil	1,293,820
Kirkuk	864,351

Landmarks:
- ▶ *Great Ziggurat of Ur*, Nasiriyah
- ▶ *Korek Tower,* Arbil
- ▶ *National Museum of Iraq,* Baghdad
- ▶ *Ruins of Nineveh,* near Mosul
- ▶ *Shrine of Ali Ibn Abi Talib,* Najaf

Economy: Iraq's economy is dominated by the oil industry, which provides about 90 percent of the government's revenue. In the energy sector, Iraq also produces natural gas and hydroelectric power. The nation's leading agricultural products include wheat, barley, rice, and dates, while Iraq's factories produce textiles, processed foods, and construction materials. In Iraqi Kurdistan in the northeast, tourism is a growing industry.

Currency: The dinar. In 2011, 1,166 dinars equaled US$1.

System of weights and measures: Metric system

Literacy rate: 74%

Currency

Iraqi student

Mohamed Al-Daradji

Common Arabic words and phrases:

al salaam alaykum	hello
ma' al-salama	good-bye
tisbah ala-khayr	good night (to a man)
tisbihin ala-khayr	good night (to a woman)
fursa sa'ida	pleased to meet you
Kif al-hal?	How are you?
baraka Allah bik	thank you
afwan	you're welcome

Prominent Iraqis:

Mohamed Al-Daradji (1978–)
Filmmaker

Saddam Hussein (1937–2006)
President

Nuri al-Maliki (1950–)
Prime minister

Muqtada al-Sadr (ca. 1974–)
Shi'i Muslim religious leader

Kadim al-Sahir (1961–)
Singer

Jalal Talabani (1933–)
President

To Find Out More

Books

- ▶ Arnold, James R. *Saddam Hussein's Iraq.* Minneapolis: Twenty-First Century Books, 2009.

- ▶ Carlisle, Rodney P. *Iraq War.* New York: Chelsea House, 2010.

- ▶ Fattah, Hala. *A Brief History of Iraq.* New York: Facts On File, 2009.

- ▶ Gruber, Beth. *Ancient Iraq: Archaeology Unlocks the Secrets of Iraq's Past.* Washington, DC: National Geographic Children's Books, 2007.

- ▶ Karsh, Efraim. *The Iran-Iraq War: 1980–1988.* New York: Rosen Publishing, 2009.

- ▶ Lankford, Ronnie D., ed. *The Iraq War.* Detroit: Greenhaven Press, 2011.

- ▶ Lightfoot, Dale. *Iraq.* New York: Chelsea House, 2007.

- ▶ Miller, Mara. *The Iraq War: A Controversial War in Perspective.* Berkeley Heights, NJ: Enslow Publishers, 2010.

Web Sites

- ▶ **BBC News—Country Profile: Iraq**
  http://news.bbc.co.uk/2/hi/middle _east/country_profiles/791014.stm
  For general information about Iraq in the past and present.

- ▶ **CIA—The World Factbook: Iraq**
  www.cia.gov/library/publications /the-world-factbook/geos/iz.html
  For current statistics about Iraq and its people.

- ▶ **National Geographic—Iraq**
  http://travel.nationalgeographic .com/travel/countries/iraq-guide
  For photographs of contemporary Iraq.

▶ **Nature Iraq**
www.natureiraq.org
For information about this organization and its efforts to protect and restore Iraq's natural habitats.

▶ **The Virtual Museum of Iraq**
www.virtualmuseumiraq.cnr.it
/homeENG.htm
For images and information about ancient treasures in the National Museum of Iraq.

Organizations and Embassies

▶ **Embassy of the Republic of Iraq**
3421 Massachusetts Avenue, NW
Washington, DC 20007
202/742-1600
www.iraqiembassy.us

▶ **Embassy of Iraq in Canada**
215 McLeod Street
Ottawa, Ontario K2P 0Z8
Canada
613/236-9177

▶ **Visit this Scholastic Web site for more information on Iraq:**
www.factsfornow.scholastic.com

Index

Page numbers in *italics* indicate illustrations.

Meet the Author

A GRADUATE OF SWARTHMORE COLLEGE, LIZ Sonneborn is a full-time writer living in Brooklyn, New York. She has written more than eighty nonfiction books for children and adults on a wide variety of subjects. Her works include *The American West*, *A to Z of American Indian Women*, *The Ancient Kushites*, *The Vietnamese Americans*, *Chronology of American Indian History*, *Guglielmo Marconi*, and *The Environmental Movement*. (A complete list of her books is available at www.lizsonneborn.com)

Sonneborn has written three other books for the Enchantment of the World series; two of them, *Yemen* and *United Arab Emirates*, were also about countries in the Middle East. Those two books presented a very different research challenge than *Iraq* did. For the previous books, finding good sources of information in English was sometimes difficult. But given the recent U.S. involvement with Iraq, there was, she says, "an intimidating number of good and relevant references to sift through for this book."

A far greater challenge, she says, was keeping up-to-date with the changing circumstances in Iraq. As a result, in addi-

tion to reading many books about Iraq's history and culture, Sonneborn went through more than one hundred newspaper and magazine articles to get a clear understanding of what is happening there. "Writing this book," Sonneborn explains, "made me grateful for the Internet. When I first began writing books, the World Wide Web wasn't available. All my research had to be done in the library. Many of the resources I used for writing *Iraq* would not even be available in a library today. And those that would, would be far more difficult to track down. This experience made me remember what an incredible tool the Internet is for any researcher."

Photo Credits

age fotostock: 17, 130 left (Giovanni Mereghetti), 84 bottom (Mohammed Reza Moradab), 92 (Trip);

Alamy Images: cover, 6 (imagebroker), back cover, 24 left (Images & Stories);

AP Images: 83 (Brennan Linsley), 52 (Chip Somodevilla), 35 (Ghassan al-Yassiri), 48 (Gun), 93, 107 (Karim Kadim), 53 (Maya Alleruzzo), 70 (Nabil al-Jourani), 49 (UNSCOM), 84 top (Yahya Ahmed);

Art Resource: 41 (Scala/White Images), 14 (SSPL/Science Museum), 11 (Werner Forman);

Bridgeman Art Library/Freer Gallery of Art, Smithsonian Institution, USA: 12;

Dreamstime/Sadık Güleç: 24 right;

Getty Images: 110 (Adel Al-Masry/AFP), 10, 114 (Ahmed Al-Rubaye/AFP), 61 top (Ali Al-Saadi/AFP), 123 (Ali Yussef/AFP), 79 (Chris Hondros), 36 (DEA PICTURE LIBRARY/De Agostini), 21 (Gilles Bassignac/Gamma Rapho), 47 (Karim Sahib/AFP), 30 (Lee Stocker/Oxford Scientific), 59 (Lynn Abercrombie), 102, 108 (Mario Tama), 86 (Marwan Naamani/AFP), 120 (Matt Cardy), 111 (Nicolas Asfouri/AFP), 106 (Philip Ryalls/Redferns), 68 (Qassem Zein/AFP), 109 (Roslan Rahman), 122, 125 (Safin Hamed/AFP), 118 (Spencer Platt), 74, 99, 100, 113, 116 (Wathiq Khuzaie);

Landov: 66, 126 (Ali Abbas/EPA), 54 (Ali Jasim/Reuters), 29 (Ali Mashhadani/Reuters), 121 (Azad Lashkari/Reuters), 72 (Jamal Saidi/Reuters), 64 top (Kahtan Al-Mesiary/Reuters), 98 (Khidar Abbas/EPA), 65 (Mohammed Ameen/Reuters), 124 (Mushtaw Muhammad/Reuters), 75 (Oleg Popov/Reuters), 57 (Patrick Baz/Reuters), 51 (Peter Andrews/Reuters), 64 bottom (Slahaldeen Rasheed/Reuters), 50 (Stefan Zaklin/Reuters), 67 (Thaier Al-Sudani/Reuters), 96 (Yannis Behrakis/Reuters);

Media Bakery/Jean-Blaise Hall: 119;

Minden Pictures/Simon Colmer/NPL: 28;

Nature Picture Library/Hannes & Jens Eriksen: 31;

Newscom: 105 (AFP/Getty Images), 33 (Ahmad Al-Rubaye/AFP/Getty Images), 63 (Ali Haider/EPA), 56 (Jim Watson/AFP/Getty Images), 34 (Jonathan Alcom/ZUMA Press), 95 (Karim Sahiba/AFP/Getty Images), 112 (Roger L. Wollenberg/UPI), 104, 133 bottom (Sakis Mitrolidis/AFP/Getty Images), 97, 132 top (Stewart Innes/ZUMA Press), 7 top, 23 (ZUMA Press);

Photo Researchers: 39 (George Gerster), 43 (Sheila Terry);

Shutterstock, Inc.: 38 bottom (John Said), 73, 132 bottom (sydeen);

Superstock, Inc.: 103 (age fotostock), 7 bottom, 32, 87 bottom, 90 (imagebroker.net), 117 (Marka), 38 top (Museum Boymans Van Beunningen, Rotterdam, Netherlands), 18, 131 bottom (National Geographic), 2, 89 (Robert Harding Picture Library), 77 (Science Faction);

The Granger Collection: 8 (Ambrose Dudley), 45 (ullstein bild), 87 top;

The Image Works: 22 (AAAC/Topham), 94 (Caroline Penn/Impact/HIP), 80 (Janet Wishnetsky/HIP), 26 (Press Association), 61 bottom, 62, 131 top (Probst/ullstein bild), 88, 133 top (Shehzad Noorani/Drik/Majority World), 13 (The British Library/Heritage).

Maps by XNR Productions, Inc.